"Every CEO should recognise the imperative of having a full diversity and inclusion program – one which acts and not just pays lip service to the politic. It is a path on which CEOs will face personal challenge, apprehension and will benefit from much learning and support from a wide range of sources to build good foundations. Leila and her amazing company, Dial, are one of those foundations. With her drive and enthusiasm and breadth of knowledge she set out to transform how CEOs work together. She shares this journey (and so much more) alongside insights from a rolodex of contacts making it one of the essential reads for all CEOs."

Steve Rowe, Former, Chief Executive Officer, Marks & Spencer Group PLC

"Diversity is crucial if we are to demonstrate that all are served within employment law within our national and international ecosystems. If our policies and process do not robustly reflect the diversity of the communities in which we serve, credibility will be lost and respect will diminish amongst those who are not being represented equitably. Equally, representation at the top is key if we are to serve as beacons for future generation of leaders to have hope that the corporate world welcomes their talent with open arms and that talent can transcend far and wide no matter what the background.

I would encourage my fellow legal practitioners to read this book as it shines a light on why we must continue to maintain momentum for good business through the lenses of diversity, inclusion. belonging, equity and culture."

Elia Montario, Senior Partner, Head of North West Corporate Team &
National Head of M&A, Shoosmiths

"Leila McKenzie-Delis is a true leader in the fight for a diverse and inclusive work force. This book is a must-read for any executive looking to bring real change."

Akshay Nayak, Founder and CEO, Tenhaven Consulting

"Helping to drive DE&I as an advocate and ally is a special part of my role. This book is a testament to why we should all be CEO Activists and play our part to drive greater social outcomes across the board. Our communities are amazing illustrations of our purpose – to live the exceptional with soul. Leila McKenzie-Delis puts heart and soul into this book whilst generously sharing many purpose-driven leadership stories alongside the compelling business case for why diversity, inclusion, and belonging = engagement. You wouldn't explain why innovation or resilience are key to improved business performance, so why treat diversity any differently? If you are looking for practical purpose with a healthy dose of passion, then look no further."

Adrian Mardel, Chief Executive Officer,
JLR (formerly Jaguar Land Rover)

"CEO Activism uses Leila's personal story and experience to create a powerful template for future leaders. Growing up in an industrial northern town as a second-generation British Pakistani, and the youngest of six children, I am passionate about social mobility and levelling the playing field for the talent of tomorrow. Business has a critical role to play in delivering a better and more inclusive future, and Leila shares her experience and advice generously to support leaders in creating positive change."

Aki Hussain, Group CEO, HISCOX and
Non-Executive Director, Visa Europe

"Leila provides a compelling vision for CEOs as champions of diversity, equity, and inclusion within the realm of ESG. An essential read for frankly anyone with an interest in doing better in this space."

Andrew Neal, Chief People Officer, Nash Squared

"Leila has taken complex and sometimes taboo subjects and talks directly to them. Taking inspiration from her approach – as leaders, we should step back and see how we too challenge our beliefs and change our default approaches to drive meaningful change, not only within our organisations but also in broader society."

Anisa Missaghi, Chief Corporate Affairs & Sustainability Officer, pladis Global

"Leila McKenzie-Delis effectively articulates the business case for prioritising diversity, equity, and inclusion within corporate sustainability strategies, offering actionable insights and inspiring examples of CEO activism."

Antonio Bebba, DE&I Europe Lead, Pfizer

"At a time when trust in politicians is at an all-time low, and social tensions are rising, this book is a timely reminder of the role good business can play in making the world a better place – and make a profit."

Ben Page, CEO, Ipsos

"*The CEO Activist* has helped me to better recognise the hidden barriers and intersectionality within our teams. Leila's strategies will help businesses to become more aware, diverse, and inclusive, allowing them to access significantly more talent, which will drive shareholder value in the long term."

Caroline Keeling, Group CEO, Keeling

"This book brilliantly guides CEOs and C-suites on integrating DEI principles into their ESG strategies and, vitally, how meaningful change accelerates businesses at all scales."

Cassius Taylor-Smith, EMEA Chief Marketing Officer, Colliers

"Change requires courage, so this is an essential read for anyone committed to building a more just and inclusive world."

Chris Glass, Global Director DEI, Soho House

"A treasure trove of real-world case studies that illustrate how CEOs can effectively champion DEI in their organisations."

Chris Williams MBA, Global Director – Diversity,
Equity & Inclusion, CBRE

"Lelia exemplifies exceptional dedication to social justice, with her work in global DEI research serving as both a catalyst and a poignant reminder of our collective responsibility. Her efforts underscore the imperative to utilize our positions of influence to foster equity and celebrate diversity. This book is a must read. I am profoundly influenced by Leila's significant contributions and am privileged to collaborate with Dial Global in our shared commitment to making substantive progress in these critical areas."

Cindy Tyeskey-Gage, Senior Vice President,
Global Employee Relations, Salesforce

"I'd encourage anyone who has the privilege to make a difference for the good, in whatever capacity to read this book. Leadership isn't a title but a combination of behaviours that lead to positive outcomes and this demonstrates that we all have the gift to be CEO activists."

Claire Livesey, People Director, British Cycling

"Leila McKenzie-Delis masterfully illustrates how CEOs can leverage their platforms to drive social change, fostering a culture of belonging and equity within their organisations while delivering value to stakeholders. This book really serves as a call to action for leaders to harness their influence for social good, driving positive change both within their organisations and beyond."

Claire Parker, Global Head of Diversity, Equity & Inclusion,
Jaguar Land Rover

"Real, practical insight into the ten facets of inclusion to ensure leaders can advocate and drive an inclusive culture and ensure everyone can be the best version of themselves in the workplace and beyond."

Dean Curtis, Chief Executive Officer, LexisNexis Risk Solutions,
Data Services at RELX, NED, Trustee & Advisor

"Capitalism has driven the global economy for the last two hundred years. The key feature of this has been profits at all costs. This has led to the damage of not only our climate but also to our well-being and our communities. Leila McKenzie-Delis offers in this remarkable book insights and strategies CEOs can use to put the 'S' into ESG. Thoroughly recommended and a good read."

Dr Sangaralingam Ramesh, Tutor UCL, PhD,
SFHEA, Qualitative Research

"Three key words in the Booth's purpose are Authentic, Caring and Responsible. How many times do we hear about political leaders being 'in power' when what we all need them to do is take responsibility? Being a CEO is not about gaining the keys to the board bathroom but being there for everyone in the organisation and Leila's book encapsulates all the human qualities that enable today's enlightened CEOs to lead great businesses."

Edwin Booth CBE DL, Executive Chairman,
E.H. Booth & Co. Ltd.

"This book is essential reading for leaders seeking to make a positive impact on society while driving sustainable business innovation and growth."

Elena Richards, Americas Chief Diversity Equity &
Inclusion Officer, KPMG

"I highly recommend *The CEO Activist: Putting the S in ESG* to anyone interested in the intersection of business, social impact, and DEI."

Emma Padmore, Colleague Engagement Lead – Vice President –
Diversity, Equity & Inclusion, Barclays

"*The CEO Activist* is not just a book—it's a manifesto for change. Leila McKenzie-Delis's impassioned plea for diversity and inclusion reminds us that at the heart of every successful organization lies a commitment to culture. Through storytelling and candid interviews, McKenzie-Delis invites readers to join her crusade, turning the tide toward a future where every voice is heard, and every individual is valued."

Eric Mosley, Founder and CEO, Workhuman

"Essential reading for CEOs and sustainability professionals committed to building a more equitable and inclusive world."

Helen Webb, CPO, WHSmith plc

"This book serves as a call to action for leaders to harness their influence for social good, driving positive change both within their organisations and beyond."

Jane Storm, CPO, easyJet

"A must read for anyone looking to improve the world (of work). Leila is a powerhouse, truly activating CEOs to understand the value of inclusion, and how to use their platform to drive positive, sustainable change."

Jasmine Hudson, Chief People Officer, Mitie

"Leila McKenzie-Delis's *The CEO Activist* is not just a book; it's a manifesto for a new era of leadership. Through her personal journey and insightful analysis, she illuminates the vital intersection of diversity, inclusion, and culture in the modern workplace. For marketers and communication leaders, this book is essential reading, offering action-able strategies to drive meaningful change and foster true belonging. Get ready to be inspired, challenged, and empowered to become the CEO Activist your organization needs."

Jen Whelan, Chief Marketing and Communications Officer,
SmartMedia Technologies

"This book illuminates the transformative power of CEOs and leaders who embrace activism as a driving force for change. Through compel-ling narratives and insightful analysis, it underscores the pivotal role of corporate activism in addressing pressing societal issues. With practical stories and strategies, Leila challenges and inspires readers to harness their influence for meaningful impact. A must read for those seeking to navigate the intersection of business and social change with courage and conviction."

Jhumar Johnson, Chief of Staff, The Open University

"This book is central to how we need to really sit up and listen to what is happening around us and how we can as leaders take affirmative action for the greater good of all society. Leila has a way of bringing her own story and that of others so brilliantly to life, it feels like you're living it with her. As a life-long HR professional and huge social mobility advo-cate, this book is something I will be referring my friends, family and colleagues to."

Jo Carlin, Senior Vice President HR Europe, Global Head of
Inclusion and Diversity, Firstsource

"Leila is a trailblazer, a superhuman being and is someone that not only has insightful lived experiences but is also able to powerfully articu-late the need for leaders to be role models and effect change. So many inequalities exist in our society and the need for difficult conversations, advocacy, and actions has never been greater. It has been a privilege to be one of the founding Dial Global CEO Activists, but I still have so much to learn and this book will be a great read for anyone that is curi-ous about the positive effects that social purpose-led behavioural change within a corporate ESG structure can bring."

Jon Dutton OBE, CEO, British Cycling, Board Member,
2023 UCI Cycling World Championships,
Major Events Panel Member, UK Sport

"In *The CEO Activist: Putting the S in ESG*, DEI isn't an afterthought; it's at the forefront of responsible leadership. This book equips CEOs with the knowledge and strategies to authentically integrate DEI principles into their ESG frameworks, empowering them to be true agents of social change."

Joslyn Dumas, I&D Program Manager, Elsevier

"A timely reminder of the immense potential CEOs hold in shaping a more sustainable and just world."

Julie Abraham, CEO, Richer Sounds

"This insightful book provides practical strategies and compelling examples of how CEOs can integrate DEI principles into their ESG initiatives, driving positive social impact while enhancing long-term business success."

Kari Daniels, CEO, SSP UK & Ireland,
Non-Executive Director, Topps Tiles

"An enlightening and empowering resource for leaders committed to driving positive change."

Kathy Presto, Chief Procurement Officer, HH Global

"In the ever-changing world that we live in, people want to feel included and that they belong. People do not leave companies; they leave poor leadership and bad culture. Leila's book is one that all C-level executives need to read.

Leila is the CEO and founder of DIAL Global, an organization that supports many of the world's biggest companies to drive DEI&B. To be an inclusive company, it has to start at the top. If the CEO and executive team are modeling the behavior, the rest of the organization will follow.

Leila and team have gathered insights annually from the biggest global companies and bring these insights to you."

Kelly Nagel, Former President GN Audio, Global Technology
Leader and Inclusion advocate and board member

"Leila's book is a must read for every leader who seeks to drive scalable impact on diversity, equity, and inclusion interpersonally and institutionally – within themselves, their teams, organisations, and society."

Lauren von Stackelberg, Chief Diversity & Inclusion Officer and Global of Wellbeing, The LEGO Group

"A few years ago, Diversity, Inclusion and Belonging were nice to haves, buzzwords, cherries on the cake. Today it is impossible to be sustainably successful without them being an intrinsic part of everything you do in business, from attracting and recruiting talent, to developing a product, to building lasting partnerships with customers and suppliers, and credibility with your Board. This book will help you ensure your strategies in this critical area land and create value.

Leila is a massive force for good and for change, but always with a weather eye on results and value. She generously uses her own story, and her increasing band of activists to drive home a focus on action and measurable results."

Liz Benison, Chief People and Transformation Officer, ISS A/S

"This book is important as it resets the landscape for discussion and reflections and thought leadership around DEI in a wider and deeper landscape, bringing a CEO viewpoint but also a lot of specialist knowledge that will help give truth to many of the areas and dimensions of diversity being spoken to, this book will help practitioners to set out a wide ambition to delve deep into many areas.

Leila is a true inspiration having experienced many of the challenges herself as a woman with a South Asian background, setting out a new and multifaceted way of looking and experience and helping us all to move forward and to learn and innovate. She is fearless and open which is a great combination to help build a great coalition."

Margot Slattery, Global Head of Diversity and Inclusion and Social Sustainability, ISS A/S

"Leila McKenzie-Delis offers a ground-breaking perspective for CEOs, sustainability and communications professionals committed to building a more just and inclusive world."

Mariana Agathoklis Schlock, Head of Communications and Employee Engagement, Verizon

"This book is a critical resource for current and future leaders who are serious about building a truly diverse workplace. The powerful narrative of Leila's life serves as both an inspiration and a driving force for meaningful change. The book shares authentic challenges faced by Leila and other professionals, along with actionable strategies to address them. It demonstrates that businesses embracing true diversity don't just compete—they lead, as it is in this environment that optimal performance effortlessly emerges."

Michael Truluck, Chairman of Joe Browns

"Bold, heartwarming, powerful and inspiring candor. Leila discusses all of the things we face as humans at the intersections of our various identities. She embraces the challenges of life and uses it as fuel for transformation. She is a prominent voice in the global business landscape, using her privilege and power to influence change and reframe how people view DEIB. For anyone questioning the importance of DEIB and ESG, this book is certainly a way to shift their perspective."

Misty Gaither, Vice President of Global Diversity, Equity, Inclusion & Belonging, Indeed.com

"*The CEO Activist* looks to bring us back to the real human and economic imperative to create organisations that can harness the full potential of people with backgrounds as diverse as the society in which we all live. It is a worthwhile read for any leader of people.

Leila has been tireless in her pursuit of better organisations through creating more diverse, equitable, and inclusive workplaces. I have been nothing short of impressed with her passion, her convening power, and the force of energy she brings to every engagement."

Nathan Coe, CEO, Auto Trader Group plc

"The businesses CEOs lead often have billions of pounds of revenues, thousands of employees and millions of customers and we know that when a leader points those assets to delivering change, they can be as powerful as any organisation globally.

How business leaders become that Activist CEO is not easy but there is nobody I have met in a 30-year career in the public and private sector who understands better how that can happen than Leila.

Her knowledge, networks, and expertise are peerless so to have that captured in this book is powerful and, frankly, a guide for anyone who wants to make a difference."

Paul Gerrard, Campaigns, Public Affairs & Board Secretariat Director,
Co-op, Trustee, Co-operative Heritage Trust

"The leadership tone must be set from the top, and our CEOs are typically the genesis of that. It's in everyone's interests to make work work. It is a marker of cultural competence and inclusion in the workplace and societal progress beyond it – all in an age where the future of work continues to unfold. Leila's network with the C-suite has given her a unique perspective to share. It's worth your investment in time to read this."

Raj Verma, Chief Diversity, Culture + Ex Officer, Sanofi

"A groundbreaking exploration of the pivotal role CEOs play in advancing diversity, equity, and inclusion as part of their ESG agenda."

Rajiv Malhotra, President EMEA Business, Managing Director &
UK Board Member, Firstsource & Exec Sponsor (WIN)
Women Inspiration Network

"I'm excited about the publication of *The CEO Activist*. This an important book, with guidance that is perhaps more important now than ever before. Having served as chief diversity officer for two of the world's largest companies, I know how important CEO activism is for any company seeking to make meaningful, measurable, and sustained progress in DEI.

There is no one better placed than Leila McKenzie-Delis to bring this to life. Her own lived experiences, her work as Founder and CEO of DIAL Global, and her extraordinary ability to convene leaders around this important subject – from boardrooms to No. 10 Downing Street – combine to make her uniquely qualified.

This book is a must read for anyone serious about diversity, equity, and inclusion. Whether you are a sitting CEO, an aspiring CEO, an advisor to CEOs, or a DEI practitioner, you will gain valuable insights, clear guidance, and inspiration from this work."

Ray Dempsey, Jr., Retired Chief Diversity Officer,
Barclays Former Chief Diversity Officer BP America,
Founder and Principal, Dempsey Inclusion Group, LLC

"Leila has a a huge amount of experience of liaising with CEOs and senior leadership, and I am looking forward to reading this book."

Rishi Chouhan, CEO, Luxury Living Homes International

"A compelling vision for CEOs as champions of diversity, equity, and inclusion within the realm of ESG."

Roisin Mackenzie, Chief People Officer, Saga plc

"In my position, so much of our teams' work is about creating environments that let people thrive. That's the beginning and then, on top of that, it is seeing a view of the future, where the workforce is this diverse and vibrant place that replicates the world in which our company operates and helps teams navigate a way to work together whilst living our differences. This book by Leila offers so many insights and personal stories from leaders in all types of roles that inspire me to keep on striving for this goal. Her experience leading DIAL, working with organisations all across the world, has meant that she has become an expert in her field and a go-to person for organisations like ours to turn to for support."

Salma de Graaff, Chief People Officer, Skyscanner

"An inspirational and thought-provoking book with insightful anecdotes from the UK's top business leaders. The author authentically shares the complexities of diversity and inclusion and offers practical solutions. A must read for any authentic leader!"

Samantha Allen, Managing Partner, Sam Allen Associates
Global Executive Search

"A diverse and inclusive work environment and team is an absolute necessity for success in today's business world and Leila McKenzie-Delis's book is a 'must read' for EVERY business leader – not just CEOs or aspiring CEOs. It is filled with data to inform and educate, interviews and stories from real-world industry executives to inspire, bring strength and ideas and a way forward to help leaders bring about real impact in business through DE&I."

Sanjiv Gossain, GM and Head of EMEA, Verizon Business

"A must read, with practical strategies for any senior leader looking to embrace a culture of belonging and equity within their business, to build an environment where everyone can strive, and ultimately deliver superior business performance."

Sophie Dekkers, Chief Commercial Officer, easyJet

"The Social juice is definitely worth the squeeze!"

Steve Murrells CBE, Group Chief Executive Officer, Hilton Food Group Plc, Non-Executive Director Noble Foods Ltd.

"This is a must read not only for every CEO but for every leader who is committed to truly creating and nurturing a diverse work environment. Leila's own personal story is powerful and she's used her story to drive change for all. She gives us data that defines the problem and she gives us tools to solve the problem. A diverse culture is much more than having representation, it's about creating an environment where people feel embraced regardless of age, gender, ethnicity. And, in belonging, top performance is achieved!"

Tami Erwin, Former EVP & CEO Verizon, Board Director, John Deere, F5, Xerox, York Space Systems and Skylo and an Operating Partner for Digital Gravity

"Diversity, equity and inclusion are critical for businesses to reflect their colleague and customer base, and to succeed in the modern world. Leila's important work not only helps us to learn from each other but also challenges us to collectively do better for the world in which we operate."

Shirine Khoury-Haq, Group CEO, Co-op

"In her new Book The CEO Activist - Putting the S in ESG Leila brings that essential combination of passion, insight and expertise to the areas of Diversity, Inclusion, Belonging, Equity and Culture but it is the passion which makes this a remarkable piece of work. This is essential reading for all leaders, whether that be of a company, or a country. Leila has written this book at a time of great uncertainty and concern in the world. Global stability seems to have been put on hold as we all struggle with domestic economic headwinds, geo political conflict, rising global tensions, climate change, AI and general mental health issues.

The underlying cause of course is often a lack of understanding and appreciation of difference, of other's perspectives on the world. This book, as well as supporting CEOs in the workplace, throws an important light on the wider global issues and in that is hugely valuable. In bringing so many rich insights from leading CEOs the book is routed in the practical and real world. Leila takes a holistic view of Diversity, Inclusion, Belonging, Equity and Culture. Her 10 facets differentiate this book from others which makes it all the more important and valuable. Whatever your role in society this book shines a light on how to create a better company, a better place, a better world. And for that we owe Leila a debt of gratitude."

Gary Browning, Advisor and Non Exec Director to the talent sector

The CEO
Activist

The CEO Activist

Putting the 'S' into ESG

Leila McKenzie-Delis

WILEY

Registered Office(s)
John Wiley & Sons, Inc., 111 River Street, Hoboken, NJ 07030, USA
John Wiley & Sons Ltd, The Atrium, Southern Gate, Chichester, West Sussex, PO19 8SQ, UK

Editorial Office
The Atrium, Southern Gate, Chichester, West Sussex, PO19 8SQ, UK

For details of our global editorial offices, customer services, and more information about Wiley products visit us at www.wiley.com.

Library of Congress Cataloging-in-Publication Data is Available:

ISBN 9781394226894 (Cloth)
ISBN 9781394226917 (ePDF)
ISBN 9781394226900 (ePub)

Cover Design: Wiley
Cover Images: © Mighty/Adobe Stock Photos, © Mike/Adobe Stock Photos, © Olena /Adobe Stock Photos
Author Photo: Courtesy of the Author
Printed and bound by CPI Group (UK) Ltd, Croydon, CR0 4YY

C9781394226894_040624

This book is dedicated to my late father Roderick John McKenzie who I miss every day. You are the original CEO Activist and always said that as long as I tried my best, then nothing else matters. You and Mum are the North Stars in my sky and have shown me the way when I haven't known myself.

Special thanks to my dedicated husband and partner in life, Costa, my wonderful mum, Anne, dearest brother, Michael, sister-in-law, Meenu, and our beautifully diverse respective families.

Gratitude to the special people, true friends, and inspirations who have been so supportive on this journey of life and business. You know who you are – I am forever indebted and grateful to you for believing in me and giving me a chance.

Last but never least – forever our baby, Peter Costa Roderick McKenzie-Delis. You have shown us that love has no boundaries. You give us hope and faith for the future generations of leaders to come.

Dad helped me proofread my first book – Diversity, Inclusion and Belonging – A leadership guide about why everyone matters and how to make them feel like they do.

My dad, mum, brother and me.

My brother Michael and me. This was taken at the old Inmarsat Offices where my brother worked before the company became Viasat.

Our family on our wedding day.

We are proud of our mixed-race baby and want him to learn about all aspects of his family heritage and culture. As the son of a potato farmer this picture is a keeper!

Scattering Dad's ashes at the top of the peak in Hong Kong. He has a wonderful view and I believe he continues to watch over us every day.

Contents

Foreword

Stephanie Mehta

In recent years, as corporate diversity, equity, and inclusion (DEI) programmes have faced criticisms from some shareholders and politicians, many executives have defended these initiatives by dispassionately making the business case for DEI. They'll trot out data that show the stock performance of companies with high levels of inclusion outpace their less-diverse peers, or they'll rationalise DEI as a tool to attract a new generation of talent that prizes a workplace that mirrors the outside world.

Leila McKenzie-Delis is putting the passion back into the discourse on diversity. In *The CEO Activist*, McKenzie-Delis shows us that equality at work isn't just about fiscal responsibility. Her book is a full-throated reminder that fostering an inclusive corporate culture simply is the right thing to do.

Make no mistake, *The CEO Activist* clearly explains the economic justification for diversity through case studies and by citing research. Knowing that companies need to "measure it to manage it", McKenzie-Delis's firm, DIAL Global, helps organisations gauge their cultures on ten facets of diversity: race, gender, sexual orientation, disability, age, mental health, parenthood, nationality, religion, and socio-economic status. McKenzie-Delis understands that a strong diversity and inclusion agenda typically needs to align with broader corporate goals and priorities.

But her quest for equality is deeply personal. *The CEO Activist* is propelled by intimate stories of McKenzie-Delis's upbringing as a person of Chinese descent, adopted by British ex-pats in Hong Kong, struggling with dyslexia. Her journey to find a holistic sense of belonging and acceptance has fuelled her professional zeal for workplace diversity.

I share McKenzie-Delis's unbridled enthusiasm for creating more equitable workplaces, and like McKenzie-Delis, my passion grew out of personal experiences. My first full-time job in journalism came via a programme that aimed to bring more minorities into newsrooms. I got my next job at *The Wall Street Journal* because I met a recruiter at a conference for Asian American journalists. Having been the beneficiary of diversity programmes, I feel a deep commitment to "pay it forward" by advocating for diversity everywhere I've worked.

McKenzie-Delis and I are not alone. *The CEO Activist* is filled with interviews with executives who share our passion for inclusion. McKenzie-Delis highlights leaders who have experienced discrimination themselves or in their families, and who can articulate the moral and ethical imperative of empowering an inclusive workforce. Their heartfelt stories arguably are more powerful than spreadsheets and charts making the business case for DEI.

And that's the thing about passion – it transcends and supports the rationale. Leila McKenzie-Delis is hardly the first person to make strong arguments for diversity. DIAL Global is neither the largest nor it is the most prominent consultancy doing work in this area. But it was McKenzie-Delis's passion that convinced me to hear her out; I dare say, dear reader, it will do the same for you.

Introduction

I really want you to think back to a time when you felt excluded. When you felt you didn't belong, you weren't wanted or your opinion was irrelevant. Maybe, like most people, it was at primary school where ever-fluctuating friendship circles dictated our quality of life. Perhaps in senior school there was a teacher who demeaned you and crushed your spirit, or it's possible you've been trapped in a toxic and bullying work environment.

I truly hope you've never felt excluded, worthless, or an outsider – and for most people who have, hopefully, these feelings stem from temporary or fleeting interactions.

Now imagine if being excluded was the default setting of your life. Not necessarily presented in the overt bullying we witnessed at school, but in subtle signals you've received your entire life that you're somehow "different".

I'm Leila McKenzie-Delis and I'm the founder and CEO of DIAL Global – an organisation that works with businesses to help them "do well, by doing good". We support their economic growth and innovation by working with them to build inclusive cultures, help them understand why diversity is critical, and demonstrate how to drive faster change at all levels.

You may wonder why I have become an expert in diversity, inclusion, belonging, equity and culture (DIBEC) and what qualifies me to write this book. Well, over the coming chapters I will share with you my story – from an orphanage in Hong Kong, to being a dyslexic child in an English high school, to having white British parents, to always being overlooked by corporate organisations intake programmes, to becoming a mother, to losing my father, to building one of the most unique and important businesses in the UK.

I will explain my own experiences of exclusion, and what I've learned from my front row seat in the fight for equity and equality in the UK.

I may be sitting here now as a founder, CEO, wife, mother, grieving daughter, leader, diversity champion and someone who has been lucky enough to build a profile and a career where I am making my mark on the world, but believe me – much of my life I have felt "different", like I don't belong, and like I will never find my place or my purpose.

In fact, if I'm being completely honest with you, I can still feel like that.

There have been times even while I've been writing this book, when I haven't felt that I've belonged in my own organisation.

Now, of course, there so many reasons why "feeling different" can happen. Sometimes it's internal factors – for example, the mood we are in, especially if we are prone to a more melancholic outlook. Sometimes it's because something seismic happens which changes our sense of self entirely.

But usually, people feel different because of external factors. The outside world is telling us that we're on the back foot because of our gender, race, sexuality, identity, socio-economic background or faith.

Do you believe that everyone should have the opportunity to fulfil their potential in the workplace – and beyond? Do you believe that every organisation can realise the benefits of inclusion? Do you believe that talent is everywhere and opportunity is not?

If you picked up this book, then I would think your answer is yes.

Are you aware that businesses which embrace having a diverse and inclusive workforce, and nurture their talent, increase profitability by at least 35%? If you didn't know that, then I'm very much looking forward to sharing with you during the course of this book, how it's down to all of us (whether we are a CEO or not) to ensure where we work, where we spend our money and the communities in which we live truly understand that building a diverse and inclusive world isn't just the right thing to do, it is a proven lever for economic growth and prosperity.

And I should know.

As part of our work supporting companies and leaders to thrive financially and morally, we focus on our ground-breaking ten holistic facets of visible and invisible diversity, including race and ethnicity, gender, sexual orientation, disability, age, mental health, parenthood and caring responsibilities, nationality, religion and socio-economic status.

We are strong believers in the phrase "you have to measure it to manage it", so we also help diagnose organisations with where they are on their diversity, inclusion, belonging, equity and culture (DIBEC) journey, and produce The DIAL Global Diversity Review – the most comprehensive review of corporate practices against the ten facets of workplace diversity and inclusion.

The research creates an industry-standard diagnostic, and delivers annual reports from the UK and the US, by tracking and measuring annually the progress of diversity, inclusion and belonging. This allows organisations to benchmark against other organisations, learn about leading practice through case studies, and set tangible goals to move the dial year-on-year.

Through my work as a diversity champion, I have many platforms to make myself heard. I run a successful company which not only make an impact in it's own right but also present me with the opportunity to comment on issues of which I'm passionate about – either in the media, or on panels or as a keynote speaker. I lead the direction for our newsletter, podcast, and, of course, social media platforms.

But it wasn't always this way. I spent many, many years lost, confused, and seeking direction. I didn't know what was wrong, or why, but I knew I wasn't living up to my potential. The dial was set to the wrong frequency and the signal was breaking up.

I've had a burning urge to get this story, my story, out into the world – because I know first-hand what it's like to be reduced to a box on a piece of paper. To feel defined by skin colour, ethnicity, and perceived impairment. I wanted to write this book because I wanted to share my journey, to impart some of the lessons I've learned, and hopefully inspire, educate, and motivate others.

But I also feel that even though every single thing that I do all day, every day, is around diversity, inclusion, belonging, that there's a big part of me which is hidden.

As my company grows, as my profile in this sector grows, I find myself telling my story over and over, time and time again. And it's an honour to be asked. To be relevant. To be heard.

But it's also made me quietly reflect, question and revisit my life so far – the experiences which have shaped me, and the ever-burning issue for anyone "different" – my identity.

Living in Britain as a minority member can be exhausting. Being asked "Where are you really from?" and having your accounts of discrimination overlooked, doubted, and often openly disputed. Being a wheelchair user and working in an organisation where the most basic needs and simplest of requests are overlooked, limiting your ability to thrive at your job. Coming from a working-class background, where your start in life, through no fault of your own, overshadows and limits what you can achieve for *the rest of your life.*

Over the last few years we've heard much of the phrase "white privilege". While I question the helpfulness of the use of the word "privilege" as it implies a wealth or ease of life that many, many white Brits do not benefit from, I do believe the race campaigner John Amaechi summed it up perfectly. He says white privilege is "the absence of inconvenience and the absence of an impediment".

And, of course, we can extend this notion far beyond the colour of our skin. It can apply to gender, sexuality, faith, physical and mental health. It's the ability to go through life navigating the social structures and experiences with ease, because they were made by and for people in your image. It's understandable therefore, that if you've lived your life existing within the structures that don't openly work against you, you may well be blinkered to how limiting a life outside these norms can be.

So why am I telling you all this?

Because I think we all have a responsibility to make a change. As individuals, as members of our communities, and as part of the workforce. This, at times, can feel like an impossible task.

I think the whole journey and the whole ethos behind the exploration of diversity, of wealth, of what the "S" in the ESG equation is (i.e. Social), lead the way to a whole number of other searching questions. For me, personally, the CEO Activist is each and every one of us because we all have it within us.

And what does activism even mean? I quite like the fact that activism is quite a controversial word because people talk a lot about how activism is negative or ignites a feeling of fear of intense change.

Simultaneously, there are plenty of positive connotations around activism, which are, "we're standing on a soapbox right now because we care". This is about the future generations of leaders. This is about searching inside our own souls and searching for what CEO Activism, the Activist CEO, mean to us and to us personally as leaders.

Diversity is living, it's breathing, it's sleeping, it's eating, it's resting, it's in pain, it's starting all over again. It's breaking itself to create a new evolution – a journey that I've been on personally.

Everyone is diverse. And more so, the context of diversity is about the sum of all of the different parts. It's not just about the individual because everyone is diverse with intersectional pieces. But then also you can't have diversity unless you have a collective, ultimately.

For those of us working in diversity, inclusion, belonging, equity, and culture (DIBEC), we know that it can feel thankless, lonely, and often futile.

But whether we are CEOs or starting out on our journey in business, no matter how we identify or what our circumstances, we all have a responsibility to do our bit.

While this book will focus on leadership – my story, and the stories of other leading CEOs – what it can teach you goes way beyond the corner office and the boardroom.

And even though I've learned so many crucial lessons in my life to date, and I'm so ready to share them with you – I've also finally understood the importance of acknowledging my own vulnerabilities, and have used writing this book as somewhat of an exercise for myself. I've embraced the need to question myself, how I lead, how I run my organisation, and how I live my life.

The people I've met through writing *The CEO Activist* have all taught me a new way to view or explore an issue, and I'm grateful to all of them for their insights and lessons.

I've gone on my own journey, personally and professionally, through the pages of this book and I hope more than anything that the thinking outlined in this book will help all of us rise up, find our inner Activist CEO, and move the DIAL for change.

The CEO
Activist

1

What Is an Activist CEO?

When we hear the word "activist", we are often faced with images of rebellion or controversy. That's not what we are talking about here.

Activist CEOs are simply leaders who want to support, include, and lead from the front an organisation which is full of employees who can bring their whole, true, authentic selves to work. They know inclusive and diverse workplaces lead to economic success and want to make their world a better place now and in the future.

They are allies and they are beacons.

And they are a key part in the fight for equity in the workplace.

Until recently, CEOs, I feel, have had a bad rap. You, I'm sure, will remember the statistic from 2019 that stated then there "were more chief executives called Steve in the FTSE 100 than there were from a minority ethnic group". We hear constant rebukes and snide comments about the stereotypical CEO being "male, pale, and stale".

Don't get me wrong. We know more opportunities for non-white, non-male leaders need to be found, and I'll explain later why the boardroom needs to look very different if organisations want to survive.

However, I also feel it's lazy, rude, dismissive, and, dare I say it, far from inclusive, to overlook the contribution of such men and what they have to offer. We need to understand these are allies – some may already be doing great things for the cause, some may just not know where to start.

But no matter where you stand on this, there is no question that the role of the CEO is changing – and we can all learn from their leadership.

Over the last ten years the world has changed exponentially, and we have seen huge political and sociological upheaval, and the boundaries between politics and business have become blurred.

In the United States, we have seen Apple's Tim Cook and Starbucks' boss Howard Schulz becoming more vocal in their advocacy on a number of issues. In a piece for the *Wall Street Journal*, Bank of America's CEO Brian Moynihan said, "Our jobs as CEOs now include driving what we think is right. It's not exactly political activism, but it is action on issues beyond business."[1]

"Action on issues beyond business", I love that phrase.

Marc Benioff of Salesforce also perfectly summed up the current CEO Activist phenomenon in an interview with *Time*, saying, "Today CEOs need to stand up not just for their shareholders, but their employees, their customers, their partners, the community, the environment, schools, everybody."[2]

Some leaders have pointed to the power of the Millennial generation as a driver of change, acknowledging that morals in business matters to younger people more than ever – as both consumers and employees.

Back in 2017, global communications firm Weber Shandwick (in partnership with KRC Research) commissioned a study on CEO Activism, called "High Noon in the C-Suite".[3] It was the follow-up to "The Dawn of CEO Activism" (2016),[4] which had focused on the risks and rewards for companies when their Chief Execs use their platform to comment on "issues beyond business". The new piece of research focused on the impact of this on the Millennial generation – and found 51% of that demographic were more likely to buy from companies led by CEO Activists.

The changing political climate in the US was seen as a major factor, as Weber Shandwick's own CEO Andy Polansky said at the time:

> *Over the past 12 months, the climate in the United States has changed dramatically as business and policy have intersected more deeply than ever before.*
>
> *When dozens of CEOs spoke up about the new administration's decisions regarding issues like climate change and travel to the U.S. from select countries, for example, social media ignited, protests erupted and media attention exploded. Navigating how to communicate a company's point of view in this environment is becoming increasingly complex and important. Future generations will only pay closer attention to how companies communicate around their values when it comes to deciding where to work or who to purchase from.*

The *Harvard Business Review* has been writing on the concept of Activist CEOs for almost a decade,[5] and they put together a fascinating précis on the tactics employed by such leaders – noting that while they would be motivated by many different interests ("external, internal and deeply personal"), in the main, they relied on two types of tactics – raising awareness and leveraging economic power. Now this was a report focusing on the US, where the main battlegrounds were over specific pieces of legislation – such as Trump's immigration laws or same-sex marriage. But even though the action taken by the American-based CEOs was mainly only relevant to their country, it began to set a precedent worldwide, the consumers wanted their big and beloved brands to stand for something.

This has been backed up in the UK, by research which came out in 2019 from a joint collaboration between the University of Bath's School of Management, Imperial College London, and Audencia Business School in France.

Their study found that: "People are over 20% more likely to want to work for a company where the CEO takes a humanistic stance on a political issue unrelated to their business."[6]

What I found especially fascinating by this particular piece of research, was that it didn't matter what the background of the respondent was or whether or not the respondent even agreed with the stance of the CEO. They simply wanted to see a leader who stood for something.

This surprised the authors themselves. Andrew Crane, Professor of Business and Society at Bath University, said at the time, "We had expected people to be attracted to principled, politically active business leaders but we were surprised to find that graduates did not necessarily need to share their opinions to find them appealing."

That said, there did appear to be a very firm line drawn. Professor Christian Voegtlin from Audencia Business School noted:

> Our findings show that the positive effect of CEO activism disappears if the CEO becomes politically active to oppose humanistic values, such as when leaders speak up against same-sex marriage.
>
> People are more likely to want to work for a company with a CEO that takes no stand whatsoever than one where he or she comes out against such issues. It seems that when CEOs speak up, they should speak up for humanistic values if they want to have a positive spill-over effect for their company.

So how do organisations and CEOs navigate when to stand up and speak, and when to stay silent?

A lot of academic work has been done in this area, and much of it focuses on what the activism will mean for the company's bottom line, and, of course, its reputation. Professor Georg Wernicke has written extensively on the concept of CEO Activism, and in a study for the *Journal of Business Ethics*,[7] he made the point that on some issues (his example being Black Lives Matter), it is clear and right and organisations should speak out, however, there are some societal issues where if the connection between the brand and the cause is vague, or the message is badly executed, then more harm will be done than good.

Wernicke offered some golden rules for CEOs to follow before deciding on making very public interventions:

- Do they offer added insight? For example, do they have specific expertise which can demonstrate the implication for a suggested government policy?
- Will it be constructive or make a useful contribution? (He suggested that if it's purely "signalling", then the voice of the CEO can "contribute to polarisation".)

He also cited transparency, meaning a leader should explain why they're using their voice on the issue. One example given was, of course, when the Apple CEO voiced his concerns about LGBTQ+ education in schools, and did so by saying he was a "proud member of the LGBTQ+ community".

I recall reading an incredibly interesting piece in *Management Today* (Summer 2023)[8] on the rise of CEO Activists, sparked by a speech from Danny Mortimer, CEO of NHS Employers, who basically urged more leaders to be braver and become activists. He said what I believe, and tend to shout from the rooftops, which is businesses which embrace activism will see long-term business benefits – though he stressed this is as long as they choose an area of ESG that is relevant to who they are as a company.

In 2023, Citigroup, which became the first major Wall Street bank to appoint a woman as their CEO, Jane Fraser, introduced new diversity goals for gender, race, and sexual orientation in its workforce for 2025. They're aiming to raise global representation of women in assistant vice-president (AVP) roles to managing director (MD) levels to 43.5% in 2025 from the current 40.6% and want to elevate the proportion of Black employees in the AVP to MD ranks to 11.5% from the current 8.1%, and the percentage of Hispanic and Latino AVPs to MDs to 16% from 13.7%.

That's not to say it's always easy to put one's head above the parapet as a leader. Spare a thought for a true Activist CEO, Tricia Griffith, the head of Progressive Corporation, who recently had to defend the organisation's inclusivity programme at a shareholders' meeting in Ohio. She said, "We think it's very important to have a fair and inclusive work environment, reflect the customers we serve and for our leaders to reflect the people they lead. We believe that Diversity, Equity & Inclusion is an important part of our growth and just the right thing to do."

I applaud her for standing up for what's right.

Former TIAA CEO Roger W. Ferguson Jr. said, "It actually is economically a smart thing to do from a standpoint of business. There are more and more studies that show diversity in the boardroom, diversity in C-suites, leads to better performance both in terms profitability, stock market performance. There are many ways in which diversity is the right thing to do and the smart thing to do."

I've been reaching out to some of the amazing Activist CEOs I know, to find out how they see themselves and their roles.

Nathan Coe is the CEO of Auto Trader. He says:

Being an Activist CEO means using our privileged positions to create workplaces and cultures that enable people from all backgrounds to make their very best contribution. It requires tangible actions and initiatives and alongside accountability for seeing change over time.

As is often the case, there are many facets that resonate, given many people don't fall into one clear group. You also can't help but be moved by the stories of family, friends and colleagues that share different facets to your own. For me personally, the facets I have spent the most time on are gender and race and ethnicity.

I think a combination of events over the past few years, including the pandemic, MeToo, BlackLivesMatter, climate change and a tight labour market, has dramatically expanded the responsibilities and expectations on leaders. Delivering good results is still critical, but not enough.

It is equally important how you get those results, including the real substance of employee engagement, culture, and how you respond to events external to the organisation.

We have never drawn such a definite line between diversity and economic growth. However, the link in my mind is very clear. We are missing the contribution of large groups of people, if we can provide an environment that attracts and gets the most out of everyone, then our access to talent increases, which over the long term will create significant economic growth and broader prosperity.

Diversity, Inclusion, Belonging, Equity and Culture are about creating unity and cohesion by doing meaningful work together and embracing both our differences and that which we have in common.

Paul Kendrick is the Chairman and former CEO of Studio Retail. He told me being a CEO Activist means "being committed to doing the right thing for your customers and people to drive long-term business benefits over short-term profit focus."

Of our ten facets of diversity, socio-economic status resonates most with him. He states:

I believe we often lose sight of this when trying to get inclusivity on other facets. For example, the root cause of race/ethnic diversity can often be a poorer backgrounds with less education which affects all ethnicities. We are in danger that many of the trends post-Covid will make this social divide worse – for example, in businesses, lowest-paid colleagues will often work in stores, factories, warehouses and have no choice but to work on site, whilst better-paid colleagues seek flexibility and ability to work from home. As with all of the facets, there is no silver bullet to fix them, but raising levels of education will, over time, bring greater inclusivity as well as economic growth.

There has been significant shift over the last 10 years in businesses to do the right thing to support customers, colleagues and the wider communities in which the business operates. Businesses are judged as much on this as they are on short-term profits, as we all fundamentally believe that ultimately it drives longer-term growth and sustainability.

CEOs of the future must embrace the fact we live in a global world, and you can't afford silo thinking – you have to recognise the differences between people and see this as a positive to grow their business.

As a CEO, you realise just how much culture is driven from the top and the business will mirror your actions – you have to lead by example, don't try and sit on a pedestal but actively engage with people across the organisation to drive the change you want to deliver.

John Dutton OBE is the CEO of British Cycling. In his view:

Being a CEO Activist means being a leader, role model and champion to tackle inequalities and make a difference.

I've seen significant change in leadership over the last few years, we have a workforce that has a lower level of resilience, greater expectations and the need for leaders to adapt to a changing environment and use different skills.

There are many examples in sport where we have used diversity as a commercial lever for economic growth and prosperity – where making a demonstrable difference in hard-to-reach communities has driven economic return allowing for further investment – e.g. Rugby League World Cup 2021. Diversity, Inclusion, Belonging, Equity and Culture mean allowing people to live their best life without barriers with a sense of happiness and fulfilment.

CEOs of the future must embrace change, challenges, and a greater sense of purpose. Without challenge, there is no achievement.

Aggie Mutuma is the CEO of Mahogany Inclusion Partners and former corporate HR of Argent Foods and McDonald's. She told me that, to her, CEO Activism means "leading an organisation that is about activism, but activism in terms of making a change, taking humanity, organisations, cultural teams from one place and support a to move to a different place".

She continued:

And that place that they're moving to certainly for me, is a place that is more inclusive, a place where there's more equity, a place where every single person has the opportunity to thrive regardless of who they are.

When I say opportunity, that doesn't mean every single person is going to take this opportunity, but that everyone has an equal playing field and that they can rise and take the opportunities that they want to take and that works for them.

Of the ten DIAL facets, the one which resonates most. . ., well, I'm a black woman. So in terms of my own experience as a human being, throughout my whole life, gender and race and ethnicity have always been part of my identity and also part of the way the world engages with me.

I'm also a parent, which is not a visible facet.

Those three things are definitely in the forefront of my mind in terms of my own experience, but in terms of resonance and importance, and where my activism lies, I would say it's across all of those.

Definitely the way I've grown up, the way I've experienced the world because of my gender, my race and ethnicity, potentially caring for it, it means that I'm awake to and very alive to the different experiences of people. So, while I'm not necessarily marginalised when it comes to my sexual orientation or my potential ability/disability, they will still resonate with me and they are all things and areas of facets that I am passionate about.

I do truly believe that we're not free unless we're all free. So we're not all in a great place. We're not all thriving unless we're all thriving.

Inclusion is not just about marginalised groups, it is about everybody.

I've definitely seen a move from transactional leadership and management to humanistic leadership management, which is beautiful, absolutely amazing, and has actually set the stage for these types of conversations that we're having around diversity and inclusion. Yes, I'm definitely pleased to see that there's a lot more conversations around soft leadership and what we would have called or been socialised to understand as feminists leadership traits. Love-based leadership is the way to go.

There are enough pieces of research out there that shows that diversity – and not just having diversity, actually having inclusion and hearing those voices – does lead to economic growth and prosperity.

Ultimately what we're talking about is creating and sustaining cultures where everybody can bring their magic and their mess to an organisation, their magic and great ideas. Their insights, their way of processing information. Then that's what decisions are based on, which then means that decisions about the organisation are right for their client or potential client.

Belonging is an interesting one because depending on the individual and also sometimes depending on the type of role, belonging is not really a word that resonates or translates back easily.

CEOs of the future must embrace difference. Difference in terms of their people. So this can be their background, definitely their ways of thinking, definitely the ways of wanting to work. There are ways of processing information and making decisions, and also difference in terms of where we are in time. What we did five years ago was great and lovely, maybe perfect for that time. But the world is moving, the world is changing at such a pace that we need to be more agile. We need to be able to embrace difference, and not be scared.

So I say CEOs of the future must embrace diversity. And I guess within that, change as well.

Aggie noted to me that while there is no shortage of life lessons from leadership coaches, the one that stands out for her is "people will remember what you make them, how you made them feel." And that's really an important one.

I can get it. Remember, great leaders have had that for a long, long time. That's definitely true. As leaders, we have the opportunity to empower, to really make a difference in someone's life. We spend a lot of time at work, so, as leaders, we have an opportunity to make a big difference in someone's life. I hope leaders are inspired to and encouraged to make an awesome difference to their people.

Liz Benison, Global Group Chief People and Transformation Officer and former CEO UK & Ireland of ISS, is another leader I wanted talk to about how she sees CEO Activism. She states:

> *With my role as a CEO I carry a responsibility to help others to achieve their potential and aspirations, whatever they may be. A big part of this is levelling the playing field so that opportunities are for all, not just those for whom our world works the best. Activism for me is using my voice to encourage others to also consider what individuals need to thrive and role modelling that whenever and wherever I can.*
>
> *Gender has been an obvious place for me to advocate for change over my career, as I have been able to personally relate and use my own experiences to drive for change. However, in recent years, I have realised that an approach that says that opportunities are for all and we just need to level the playing field to allow all to thrive, works well alongside a culture of investing in understanding the unique and specific challenges each facet presents.*
>
> *The thing that gives me the most optimism in recent years is that we are starting to move away from a leadership image that has been in place for many decades if not centuries, whereby the leader was all-powerful and strong, and ultimately the go-to person for all decisions. We are now openly talking about empathy as an essential skill in leaders, of leaders needing to show vulnerability in order to engender trust, and of servant leadership, whereby the leader exists to serve the team and their market rather than being "at the top of the tree". I love all of this because it makes it easier for leaders from different backgrounds and styles to be successful, and this new diversity of thinking, I believe, will*

allow us to build far better organisations that service all of their stake-holders in a better way.

At ISS, we absolutely see social impact and diversity as a critical differentiator in bids, particularly when we are aspiring to work with public sector customers. Being able to demonstrate that our team will better represent the customers' own employees and customers, because we are able to recruit and develop talent from diverse pools sets us apart in competitive tendering.

It's a feeling – when you are excited to get to work, when you feel good in the company of your colleagues, when you know you'll be supported in achieving your goals, when you don't have to hide aspects of your life and personality – that's when you feel you belong and when you can do your best work.

What Is ESG and Why Is the "S" So Important?

ESG stands for Environmental, Social, and Governance, which are the three pillars by which we judge organisations to see how they measure up and to make sure they're operating for the good of society and the world. We're not just looking at corporations' profit margins, but rather examining and analysing what impact (good or bad) they have on the world. As Deloitte eloquently explains, "The goal of ESG is to capture all the non-financial risks and opportunities inherent to a company's day-to-day activities." This is something that I applaud and embrace.

In Chapter 2, we will do a deep dive as to why specifically diversity, inclusion, and equity are so crucial to a thriving economy, and why it's the responsibility of all of us to hold industry to account, but in the meantime, it's important to note just how seriously accountability for moral behaviour of companies is already being taken.

In April 2021, the European Commission adopted the sustainable finance package which increased its scope in reporting ESG issues, so, as of 2023, almost 50,000 companies in the EU will have to file reports on it. Not only that, it's now almost certain investors will incorporate ESG elements into their decision-making process as well.

The pillars of Environmental and Governance are pretty self-explanatory. In environmental, factors such as emissions of greenhouse gases and air, water and ground pollution are monitored, as are which resources are used in production processes. Deforestation and biodiversity disclosures are also included, as are any *positive* sustainability impacts they might have.

For governance, reporting centres on shareholders' rights, board diversity, executive pay, and corporate behaviour.

The Social Pillar is the element of corporate accountability that I am so incredibly passionate about, and where I feel I can help organisations make the biggest difference – to their bank balance, their workforce, and the wider society.

It's where they report on everything from product liabilities to supply chains and sourcing issues, to how they provide access to their products and services to underprivileged social groups, to employee development.

It's where companies are supposed to measure how they do no harm, and ideally actually do good. It's where they are supposed to say, "this is how we look after our people, our customers, our suppliers, and the marginalised groups that fall across all three, who we want to elevate, support, and stand alongside."

I recently saw an interview with Amanda Blanc, CEO of Aviva. I was impressed with her commitment to the social responsibility of organisations. "This is not a fad," she told PWC for their 25th Annual CEO Survey. "Top of our agenda is looking at how we are running the business, not just for today but for three years, five years, 10 years, 20 years' time and beyond."

"You can't just focus on leaving a legacy and forget that dividends need to be paid, and results need to be achieved today. Aviva has been in existence for 325 years and as much as investors might sometimes want us to think quarter by quarter, you cannot just think like that. You have to do the right things. I hope in another 325 years, whoever is leading this organisation can look back and say key decisions taken on ESG were fundamental in Aviva's success and longevity."

Aviva updated its ESG commitments back in 2021 and pulled no punches, now requiring all of its suppliers to prove a clear commitment to net zero by 2040. It also won't invest in or underwrite businesses where more than 5% of revenue comes from fossil fuel.

Amanda continued: "We have hundreds of billions of pounds of assets under management, we have a huge opportunity to influence where we invest. We spoke to the top 30 carbon emitters in our equity portfolio and said to them 'You have three years to sort yourself out and come up with a transition plan, otherwise we will be disinvesting.'"

Accountability is also critical to Blanc, with the company aligning 10% of its executives' incentive plan to Aviva's performance on sustainability and diversity targets. She states: "I do think accountability can move the dial on ESG. It's not the only mechanism, but having that in the scorecard shows investors we are serious about it and it shows the outside world that we are serious about it."

And, a woman after my own heart, she also said: "I am a big believer in what gets measured gets done. If all you are making is bland statements, then who can be held accountable for that?"

"Investors are also expecting to see this kind of accountability," says Blanc. "Investors are asking how our remuneration is tied to ESG targets, the same as they have always asked how our remuneration is tied to profitability."

Customers are also expecting to see big businesses accountable.

"We have around 15 million customers in the UK. You cannot have an organisation that doesn't reflect the diversity of those customers any more than you can have an organisation that ignores its role in society when it has so much money to invest."

Entain, the FTSE100 betting and gaming group run by CEO Jette Nygaard-Andersen, has a similar strategy. Speaking at one of their live events, she said: "We are determined to lead the industry on our way to sustainable growth. We see no conflict between growth and sustainability, and we can see across many markets how our business can grow responsibly."

She too thinks ESG is the key driver behind moving the industry forward. "Having spoken with innovators and competitors in our market, the global momentum towards ESG and the celebration of it are clear. Investments trends are clear – they point towards ESG." She also added a stat that I love – telling the audience that 90% of investors use ESG as a key criterion when contemplating investment and that having a high concern for ESG is a primary attraction to 25% of prospective recruits.

As Amanda Blanc said: "These commitments aren't going away. This isn't just a gesture."

Julie Sweet, CEO of Accenture, spoke at the virtual Davos gathering of the World Economic Forum during the pandemic, at a time when CEOs were focusing on protecting staff but also desperately conscious of the economic storm that was potentially around the corner.

I remember at the time being struck by her words, because I was very concerned that with so many pressures for CEOs, sustainability would be something I would need to fight hard to get leaders to prioritise.

However, Sweet said:

> *As people are re-building, re-platforming in the Cloud and investing, there's a huge interest in doing so sustainably. Consumers want it, employees want it. Research that we just did in Europe said that companies who embrace both technology and sustainability are two-and-a-half times more likely to be tomorrow's leaders. I'm very hopeful that when we have this dialogue in 2025, we'll be talking about how every business is a sustainable business.*
>
> *My message to companies around the world – and particularly CEOs – is, "The only way that we'll do this faster is if you bring parts of the company together." It's one of the reasons we switched our strategy to say, "We're going to bring the [sustainability] question at least into everything we do."*

I couldn't agree more. That's why working with companies in the UK, Europe, and the US brings me such joy and sense of accomplishment. The team at Dial Global and I guide clients through how best to build a diverse and inclusive workforce, to provide and serve a diverse and inclusive world.

The ESG "S" Framework

A project that DIAL has developed, much like the DIAL Global Diversity Review, is the ESG "S" Framework.

We've commissioned a report from two esteemed academics (more on them to come) in order to create a framework that will measure the "S" in ESG and create a global standard. It will benchmark companies in a similar way that, for example, Experian measures our credit ratings. So DIAL will be able to audit and measure the social responsibility of organisations of any size.

But where does all this start?

Buy-in from the top, and an open mind to measuring progress.

Hans Vestberg, the Chairman and CEO of Verizon, is a perfect example of that. He spoke at the The Women Business Collaborative's annual summit in 2022, telling the audience: "Our Diversity & Inclusion Strategy extends throughout our entire organization. Because effective leadership is not based on what you say but what you do, we constantly track our effectiveness and have appointed an outside auditor to tell us objectively how we are doing and how we can improve."

For me, Hans is a stand-out Activist CEO. We will hear more about him later on, when we explore the facet of race in the workplace, but for now – if you aren't aware of his work – let me tell you how impressed I was when I saw his emotional broadcast in the summer of 2020 after the death of George Floyd. There was a man so worried about what he was seeing in the world, so full of horror at those horrific scenes, he wept as he addressed his Verizon colleagues, and donated $10 million to causes fighting for racial equality.

That is a leader who "gets it".

Now, it's not always the CEO who calls on our services – often it's the Chief Diversity Officer, Chief Human Resource Officer, Chief Marketing Officer or other C-Suiters who initially see the value of our contribution – but the CEO themselves has to sign it off. They have to see our vision. They have to see the moral and business case. They have to want to lead from the front.

I've had the immense pleasure and am proud to work with some of the UK's best-known, most impressive, and most ground-breaking CEOs. Some of them will appear in this book, as they share with us their thoughts on CEO Activism. So many of them have taught me invaluable lessons – about my business, my own journey as a CEO, and about myself as well.

We have built up so many incredible relationships with our leading CEOs, many of whom are aligned with the idea they want to create change in business and in society, so in 2022 we decided to create the CEO Activist Council.

There is a huge opportunity for business to positively impact wider society, and for governments to be able to drive better policy, decision-making, and outcomes that also drive economic growth and prosperity.

The CEO Council is unique, as it's the only council in the UK that focuses on diversity as a commercial lever for economic growth and prosperity.

It's also the perfect example of how one simple idea can grow into something so much bigger than we ever imagined. Initially, DIAL Global launched the CEO Activist Pledge – many of the UK's biggest organisations came on board, promising to create more inclusive workforces across the country.

The Three Steves launched it with us – Steve Murrells, then CEO of The Co-op, Steve Rowe from M&S, and Steve Ingham from Page Group – and before long we had many more on board.

- Steve Murrells, former CEO, Hilton food Group
- Steve Rowe, former CEO, Marks & Spencer
- Steve Ingham, former CEO, Page Group
- Alan Jope, former CEO, Unilever
- Peter MacNab, CEO, Superdrug
- Andrew Denton, CEO, Alfa Financial Software
- Dean Curtis, CEO, LexisNexis Risk Solutions, Data Services at RELX
- Ben Page, Global CEO, IPSOS
- Helen Calcraft, CEO, Lucky Generals
- Buta Atwal, CEO, Wrightbus
- Mike Perez, Group CEO, HH Global
- Tony Reed, CEO, TCFM
- James Millward, MD, Eurilait
- Philip Hoggarth, CEO, Communisis
- Jon Dutton OBE, CEO British Cycling
- Niamh Furey, former MD Fresenius Kabi, now VP Commercial Operations Biopharmaceuticals EU & RoW Fresenius Kabi, Board Member British Specialist Nutrition Association, Fresenius Kabi
- Shirine Khoury Haq, CEO of the Co-op Group

I was also so kindly invited by Myles Stacey OBE, Special Advisor to the Prime Minister to conduct a series of round table breakfasts at Number 10 Downing Street where we were joined by MP's; Robert Halfon and Mims Davies where discussed the importance of diversity as a commercial lever for economic growth and prosperity. Many of these established executives I am most hopeful will also join our CEO Activist Council and continue to influence their companies and respective CEO's to support me in moving the dial in the right direction.

Attendees across our 3 mornings in 2023 included:

18th May

Lord Simon Wooley CBE, Principal at Hommerton / college Cambridge and founder of operation Black Vote

Sir Lloyd Dorfman CVO CBE, Founder of Travelex and Chair at Esselco

Aline Santos, Chief Brand Officer and Chief Equity Diversity & Inclusion Officer at Unilever

Andrew Carnie, CEO of Soho house

Ben Osborn, President International Commercial Office of Pzifer

Ben Page, Global CEO of Ipsos

Chris Mouskoundi, Director of Private Wealth at Dorfman Family Office

Gavin Lewis, Managing Director of BlackRock

Helen Webb, CPO of WH Smiths, Non-Executive Director of Battersea and Board Adviser

Jo Portlock, VP Diversity, Inclusion and Belonging at LexisNexis Risk Solutions

John Deans, Chairman (UK) Rothschild Global Advisory

John Jordan, Chief Operations Officer at Arbor Investments

Lisa Fernihough, Head of Advisory - KPMG UK

Josh Partridge, Chief Operating Officer @ Newsroom AI

Kari Daniels, Chief Executive Officer at SSP UK and Ireland

Kristian Elgey, President at HH Global

Liz Bennison, CEO, UK & Ireland at ISS

Margot Slattery, Global Head of Diversity and Inclusion at ISS

Nathan Coe, CEO at Auto Trader Group plc

Pippa Dale, Director - DCM Investment Banking Partnerships & Spark Live LSEG

Rajat Dhawan, Group Chief Technology Officer at Soho House & Co

Rapahael De Boton, Senior Managing Director at Blackstone

Ray Dempsey, Founder & Principle of Dempsey Inclusion Group LLC

Robert MacMillan, Executive Chairman at HH Global

Sam Allen, Managing Partner at Sam Allen Associates Global Executive Search

Sanjiv Gossain, General Manager & Head of EMEA, Verizon Business

Sean Haley, CEO of Sodexo UK & Ireland

Tevin Tobun, CEO & Founder, ROUTD Technology/ CEO, GV Group

Zareena Brown, CPO of Royal Mail

June 7th

Karen Walker, Contributor, Forbes, Executive Coach

Andrew Denton, Chief Executive Officer at Alfa Financial Software

Chloe Target Adams, Global Director of Race Promotion

Dean Curtis, Chief Executive Officer - LexisNexis Risk Solutions, Data Services at RELX, NED, Trustee & Advisor

Jane Storm, Group People Director at easyJet

Jhumar Johnson, Chief of Staff to Vice Chancellor at The Open University

Jon Dutton, Chief Executive, British Cycling

Mark Raban, Chief Executive Officer, Lookers PLC

Salma de Graaf, Chief People Officer at Sky Scanner

Trevor Phillips, Columnist at The Times and Presenter on Sunday Morning with Trevor Phillips Sky News

Andrew Denton, chief Executive Officer at Alfa Financial Software

Vicky Edwards, Chief People Officer at Alfa Financial Software

Elly Tomlins, Chief People Officer at BRITVIC PLC

Simon Litherland, CEO at Britvic Soft Drinks

Sophie Dekkers, Chief Commercial Officer at EasyJet

Johan Svanstrom, CEO Rightmove Plc

Euan Sutherland, CEO at AG Barr

Mark Powell, Honorary Member of the PepTalks community

Cassius Taylor-Smith, Chief Marketing Officer, EMEA at Colliers

Sanjay Bhardari, Chair at Kick It Out, Chair at Satellite Applications Catapult, Board Adviser

Dame Martina Millburn DCVO, CBE, Former CEO of The Prince's Trust

Jasmine Hudson, Chief People Officer at Mitie

Christian Horner, Team Principle and CEO, Red Bull Racing

8th June

Anisa Missaghi, Chief Corporate Affairs and Sustainability Officer at Pladis Global

Caroline Keeling, Chief Executive Officer at Keelings

Diane Lightfoot, CEO at Business Disability Forum

Nazreen Visram, Head of Charities, Public Sector, Barclays, Barclays

John Lyttle, CEO boohoo group PLC

Mike Randall, Chief Executive Officer at Simply Asset Finance

Raj Verma, Chief Diversity, Culture + Ex Officer

Salman Amin, CEO of Pladis

Michael Truluck, Chairman of Joe Browns

Jessamy Baird, General Manager, General Medicines, Sanofi UK and Ireland, Vice President at The Association of the British Pharmaceutical Industry (ABPI)

Will Stratton-Morris, Chief Executive Officer at Caffè Nero

Andrew Dalton, Chief Financial Officer at Horizon Care & Education

James Martin, Chief People Officer at Rio Tinto

Daksh Gupta, Group CEO of Huws Gray, VP of The IMI and Board Advisor to Ford of Europe

Jon Jenkins, Chief Executive Officer at Hovis

Howard Luft, Chief Executive Officer, Selco Builders Warehouse

John Duffy, Chief Executive Officer, Finsbury Foods

Steve Murrells described the Pledge as "an important step towards creating diverse and inclusive workplaces for all our colleagues where they feel a true sense of belonging. Collectively, as CEOs and leadership teams, we know that more must be done; and each of us has a responsibility to be role models and agents of change to drive true inclusion throughout our organisations, our products and services and the communities we serve."

Before long, it became clear that there was an appetite to do more, and the CEO Activist Council was born.

CEOs in business, tech, retail, professional services, and construction are coming together on a single issue. These leaders generate hundreds of billions of revenue, lead hundreds of thousands of employees, and have hundreds of years of experience – and they're joining forces with DIAL to show their commitment to making UK business more diverse and inclusive.

They can't all be wrong.

They're using their experience, expertise, and insights to ensure those making policy understand the UK needs to embrace the economic benefits of diversity and inclusion.

Paul Gerrard is the Campaigns, Public Affairs & Board Secretariat Director at the Co-op Group and one of the genius brains behind our CEO Activist Council. He told us:

> *During the pandemic, businesses suddenly realised that government, through Parliament, can affect their business in quite a fundamental way. All businesses knew that but it tended to play out in a longer time. During the pandemic and lockdowns, it actually happened in days. Businesses were prevented from trading. So the impact government, through Parliament, had on business was palpable.*
>
> *I think what businesses sometimes fail to realise is that the knowledge, expertise and insight that businesses have is unique and the government love to have access to that policy and that policy affects how businesses can go about the activities.*
>
> *If you get 25 CEOs in a room, each with 20 years' experience, each running businesses at 5 or 10 millions of pounds a year – you can do the maths. You've suddenly got hundreds of years of experience at the top end of business, running with hundreds of billions of pounds of revenue. If you don't get expertise from that and you can't draw on it, then civil servants shouldn't be civil servants and politicians shouldn't be politicians.*

Josh Partridge is the Head of EMEA, Yahoo, and a key partner in our Activist Council. According to him:

> *Having that peer set there, having the same challenges as you are, having that community of leaders is hugely valuable. I think we all are dealing with very similar issues right now. As leaders, we should be trying to get as broad a perspective on the challenges that we have, which just happen to be the same challenges as most of the other CEOs have as well.*
>
> *To create that community of leaders here in the UK, I think is really, really valuable. Rallying around a really important topic is even more important as well. When we went to Downing Street – just to see the breadth and the depth in different industries at that one table, really advocating different perspectives, but all pushing for the same, trying to achieve the same thing, was quite something.*
>
> *I think, as a leader, it's inspirational actually to hear some of the other stories and ask if maybe we're actually a little bit behind and 'do I need to push a little bit harder?'*
>
> *I think having that network of like-minded people all having that same sort of challenge is really, really important because it does inspire me. Very, very successful leaders that you are able to bring together.*

Our goal is to ensure the CEO Activist Council is seen by national decision-makers as a source they can draw on in order to make more equitable policy decisions. They are ready to help the government, future governments of whatever colour, in order to make UK business the most diverse and inclusive in the world.

It is the key to commercial success.

Notes

1. www.weforum.org/agenda/2019/02/3-reasons-why-we
2. https://time.com/4276603/marc-benioff-salesforce-lgbt-rfra/

3. webershandwick.com/uploads/news/files/ceo
4. webershandwick.com/.../the-dawn-of-ceo-activism.pdf
5. https://hbr.org/2018/01/the-new-ceo-activists#:~:text=
   Political%20and%20social%20upheaval%20has,for%
   20a%20range%20of%20causes
6. https://www.bath.ac.uk/announcements/ceo-political-
   activism-jobseekers-want-principled-bosses-who-take-
   a-stand/
7. A. Feix and G. Wernicke, When Is CEO Activism
   Conducive to the Democratic Process? *Journal of Business
   Ethics* (2023): 1–20.
8. https://www.managementtoday.co.uk/ceos-become-
   activists/leadership-lessons/article/1828688

2

Why We All Need to Be Activist CEOs

Diversity, Inclusion and Belonging – and Why They Matter

If you ever want to see someone's eyes glaze over, ask them about diversity. It's a polarising concept. Is it purely a buzz word for a new fad? Or a box-ticking exercise where under-qualified people are hired to make a point and threaten the status quo?

Clearly, the answer is none of those things.

People get really het up over it, but diversity to me is simple. It simply means "difference". Difference in terms of our backgrounds, difference in terms of our life experiences and therefore ultimately the differences which led us to be where we are, right at this moment in time. What are the experiences that led us to that point? And how have those various different life experiences ultimately shaped our thinking?

The diversity of our experiences leads to a diversity of thought processes, which – translated into the world of business – leads to a diversity in how we perceive problems or handle crises, how we can shape outcomes and how we can bring different perspectives and ideas to the boardroom, to the creative process, and to the factory floor. We are all kaleidoscopes with different visions which can create a beautiful and effective outcome when moulded together.

When people get hurt about diversity, I never fully understand. It's exclusion that's truly hurtful.

When we look at diversity, and when we look at difference, we look at everything from gender and ethnicity to socio-economic background, to religion, culture and belief systems, sexuality and sexual identity, to parenting and caring responsibilities, mental health, wellness, mindset, and neurodiversity.

Identity is a complex issue. There are the fundamental simple facts of our birth, such as gender, sexuality, and race. There are external factors such as the socio-economic situation into which we're born and raised, and then there are added layers which we experience as we grow, learn about ourselves, and have experiences which change us.

There are some elements of our identity which we put front and centre, which feel the most appropriate way to present ourselves, or are the parts of what makes us "us" which we want to show the world, and where we place the most importance. And then all the other elements tend to fall further down our list.

First and foremost, I'm a proud mother to a beautiful baby boy, who my Greek American husband and I had through IVF. I am a woman, a wife, and a sister. I'm British, though I have Chinese heritage. I'm adopted, I have dyslexia. Oh, and from time to time I have experienced crippling anxiety and depression suspected ADHD.

This is intersectionality. Where we realise and accept that we have many labels, many aspects to our being, and those separate elements occupy a different percentage of our make-up. You look at the list of identities and you pull out the ones that would relate to you.

So why is diversity important? It's important because if every single person thought the same and had the same take on every situation, then we'd always have the same outcome.

And, again, in a business context, if we look at the hierarchical systems, we see people who may look the same, but we also know that those people have very similar backgrounds and ultimately ways of thinking because of their education and their culture. The ways that they have been brought up have all been the same. Therefore, companies end up with a lack of potential innovation and a lack of representation when it comes to wider society.

To some, and that's mainly those benefiting from this system, there's really no need to rock the boat. They see no problem with not hiring in their image. Whether that's a form of short-sighted, thoughtless ignorance, or whether it's a genuinely held faith in their own superiority. However, it's widely accepted that greater diversity in the workplace results in greater profitability.

In my work as the CEO of DIAL Global, I meet, talk to, and work with many CEOs. The vast majority of them and their leadership teams know and accept that there is impressive data supporting the fact that diversity is better for business in terms of profitability, and better business in terms of engagement. Therefore, engagement equals higher productivity equals higher profit, so it's pretty simple in terms of the mathematical equations.

That said, I don't believe that the way to convince CEOs and other business leaders is purely through the numbers alone. And throwing just statistics at them has clearly not worked thus far, as while the conversations around diversity and inclusion are many, we are yet to see results flowing into the boardroom, the C-suite, and beyond.

Change has to come from the top. It has to come from the leaders themselves. And there are some incredible activist CEOs driving the movement to true diversity and inclusivity.

For any doubters questioning the importance of diversity, we need to win their hearts and minds and encourage them to see their own diversity. Everyone is diverse, and everyone has a different journey to their destination.

There is one factor in the diversity movement which is all too often overlooked. The power of equity. We talk about equality constantly. We "strive" for equality for women, for minority ethnic groups, for the LGBTQ+ community, and for people with mental health issues, physical disabilities, or other vulnerabilities. But how can we reach true equality if we fail to acknowledge the fact far too many people are starting from a point of disadvantage? If we want to get to equality, we first must recognise our equity.

It can often be a confusing concept. There's a really simple yet very smart cartoon which explains the difference perfectly.

Imagine three people of different heights trying to peer over a fence. Equality looks like them ALL having a box to stand on. The tallest person goes from having a good view to a great view. The shortest person goes from having no view, to still only peering over the top of the fence. Yet as they're all given the same box, that's seen as equality.

Then imagine the same three people peering over the fence. The tallest person can see perfectly well, so doesn't need a box on which to stand. The second person needs only one box to see, and the shortest person gets two boxes in order to see. That's equity. The end result means they all get to see, equally but measures are put in place to ensure it's possible.

As a campaigner for equality, diversity and inclusion, I've often put my head above the parapet to argue in favour of the much-derided White, male, middle-aged CEO.

Is it right that there are more men called Steve running companies in the FTSE 250 then there are women? No, of course not.

Do we need to see more varied, diverse, and thriving examples of leadership teams on corporate websites? Yes, of course we do.

But if we leave change to gradually develop from the grassroots and cross our fingers while we hope for the best, we will still be here in ten years' time.

It is often the White, male, middle-aged CEO who wields the power needed for change. It's these men that need to be our allies. It's these men who need to see change must be made, and rather than run from the challenge in order to protect their piece of the pie, accept the challenge to spearhead the move to equality by embracing the need for equity. It's the CEOs who need to be convinced by the power of diversity, and the CEOs who must have true buy-in.

If change is left to grow from only a grassroots level, then it's the equivalent of running the gauntlet with all of the challenges and hurdles in the way. Change can't be expected to flourish at a grassroots level without intervention and support.

My argument continues to be "start at the top" because you see the trickle effect and you see it happen far quicker. Having the right leader is absolutely imperative and having the right people at the top, in those coveted positions of power, who genuinely want to change this are crucial. These activist CEOs are the people who can implement these badly needed interventions in order to make sure true change filters down every single layer of a business.

My background is in recruitment, and back in my headhunting days I would hear hiring managers continually tell me "Yes, but . . .". There was so much resistance to thinking outside the box when it came to hiring different faces. I would hear time and time again, that candidate had to have the right skills, or already be in the right job while at the same time giving me poor excuses about hiring someone I'd presented because what the organisation really wanted to see was a square peg in a square hole when actually, they could have looked outside of the box.

The same people got the same jobs. They still do. But what if it was different? What if we did look outside the box?

Nobody would disagree that it's "about the skills", but I've always been excited by the possibilities that open up when you explore the candidates who have *similar* skills coupled with different cultural experiences.

And to hear that those people don't exist? I call that bullshit, because those people are absolutely out there.

Yes, candidates need to have the right qualifications, experiences, and abilities to perform in the top levels of business. But if certain groups of people are never given the opportunity to obtain those sought-after abilities, and are therefore constantly overlooked, perhaps it's time for a rethink.

I'm endlessly motivated and excited to see what could be achieved if we simply adjusted our thinking slightly, if we moved the dial a few notches . . . and just widened that net.

What vision of modern business could we build if we opened our minds, and began to consider candidates that have *some* of the skills on paper, as well as real world, cultural, life-experience based attributes as well?

The issue is, organisations don't yet value all those other attributes. They want the easy hire and the easy fix. They want the quick, safe, and the easy person that they can bring into that role, because let's be honest – who's going kick up a fuss? And, of course, "hiring diverse" can have hugely detrimental effects if it's not done correctly.

Imagine a beautiful, blank canvas of a garden with so much potential for beauty and joy. But when you're planting those precious seeds in the hope of creating something great, you fail to prepare the ground properly, so the seedlings can't thrive and grow. Businesses, like bodies, can end up with corporate "organ rejection". If they've not primed the area or the place for the knowledge to grow, then there is a very real risk of organ rejection. You put that living, breathing sleeping organ inside another organ that is completely ill-prepared to accept it, then you end up with a rejected, wasted organ. Then the body says, "Well, we did try diversity but it didn't work. So let's go back to hiring things how we did beforehand."

The answer is not one silver bullet, and it's never going to be one silver bullet. It's a multifaceted issue and we don't want to end up with "tokenistic hiring", i.e. hiring people *just because* of what they look like.

We need to realise that while perfect square pegs may fit in perfect square holes, we're never going to expand and potentially survive into the future, in an ever-changing world of business, if we don't start to do things differently.

Diversity may be the buzz word that gets everyone excited but doesn't mean much if it's not supported by inclusion, belonging, and a cultural and equitable environment that lays the foundations for individuals to be able to thrive.

Don't be put off by even more potentially airy-fairy words though. One of my still much-loved and favourite quotes by Verna Myers, former VP of Inclusion Strategy at Netflix is "diversity is being invited to the party, inclusion is being asked to dance".

To add further context:

Diversity is basically getting an invitation to the party. An invitation which is not much use if you spend the entire event in a corner, with no drink, getting sneered at by people in designer shoes.

Inclusion is getting the invite to the party, being welcomed when you're at the door, being handed a drink and asked to dance (and probably someone telling you they like your coat as well).

Belonging is the magic that happens when you're so comfortable at the party that you kick your shoes off, stay until 3 in the morning on the sofa drinking tea, and sharing your whole self and knowing that you will still be welcome. Perhaps your ideas and comments will even change someone else's way of thinking.

It's such a simple analogy but I really love it. What is the point in a business, or school, or sports club, or place of worship, saying they "believe in diversity" if anyone from a minority group in that community feels alone, unheard, undervalued, or actively discriminated against?

Now take those thoughts out of the social environment and put them in the context of a work environment.

You come to work to do a job. You want to be in surroundings in which you feel relatively comfortable. It will help you perform better in the workplace, and you will thrive rather than survive.

Now, of course, we may never be quite our "Saturday self" at work, and many people will always want to compartmentalise between their professional self and their personal self. I completely understand that not everyone wants to be vulnerable at work, share their innermost feelings or the ins and outs of their identity. However, I think we all agree that we want to bring our "good self" to work, and we want to do good work.

So, if you find you're not being included in conversations, not only would it hinder your ability to be able to do your job, it's also probably likely to cause feelings of anxiety, feelings of concern, even physical symptoms of worry. And if you're having those feelings of worry or concern, then you're not thinking about the task in hand, you're not thinking about the job.

Persistently having those feelings leads to a certain sense of disengagement, and furthermore, there may be even resentment, if you are always being excluded from every decision-making process or excluded from certain conversations.

Some 30% of people who are in the minority in a particular situation, spend 30% of their time worrying about how they fit in.

Learning that statistic was a real lightbulb moment. Imagine all of that time being lost, and think what could be achieved instead through productivity. It reminded me of my teenage years, and how we don't see our youth, our beauty, and our potential because we're adrift, lost at sea.

We are more than one element of our identities. Not only that, often those elements of our identities change over time – our very essence is fluid. Either by the decisions we actively make or by events which happen to us.

People change their gender, or make decisions to acknowledge or openly live with a sexuality they'd once kept hidden. Our marital status changes (perhaps several times!) and our mental health fluctuates. Our physical health can betray us, and our identity in relation to our caring or parental responsibilities alters over time as well.

So I prefer, then, not to think of our identities as boxes we can neatly fold ourselves away into. Instead, I invite you to look at identity as a kaleidoscope – with some images staying consistent your whole life, and others moving around, changing colour, and creating another view. And if you get the right angle, with the right perspective – it can all be beautiful.

If we start looking at identity as a gracefully moving concept, we may be able to be equally fluid when it comes to creating the inclusive society I dream of.

But, as of 2024, there is still work to be done.

If there is one thing I want to stress from the outset, it's that I don't believe in creating division. The world is divided enough. I want to create a world of unity, of shared visions, and a world where our differences are explored, discussed, heard, and embraced. I want to see a world where we can celebrate all that we have in common, and applaud and respect our differences. So it doesn't sit well with me, therefore, to endlessly point out the people who "have it good", and victimise those who've spent a lifetime being overlooked.

Is there abhorrent inequality in society? Yes.

Has the world, to date, been dominated by the achievements of White, middle-aged, middle- to upper-class men? Yes.

Back in 2019, which, granted, does feel a world away now, there was a headline from Involve stating that there were then more chief executives called Steve in the FTSE 100 than there were from a minority ethnic group.

In fact, minority ethnic groups were also under-represented in the FTSE 250 as well, and more than half of FTSE 100 companies had no ethnic minority board members, during this research period. The research reported that the UK economy was losing £2.6 billion due to such discrimination.

Does this mean that all White, middle-aged men have been handed a successful life of riches? No, of course not.

In fact, in the wake of the Brexit result in June 2016, it was the votes of the White, working-class men who had felt ignored, under-supported and overlooked their entire life which made the establishment re-address the needs of this particular socio-economic group.

Much has been said over the past few years about White, working-class school boys for whom outcomes in Britain are pretty dismal.

Back in 2015, the UK's Equality and Human Rights Commission (EHRC) stated that White, male students from poor families are getting a "worse start in life", and perform worse in GCSEs than other socio-economic and ethnic groups.

In 2020, MPs heard evidence from Professor Matthew Goodwin who told the group investigating underachievement among disadvantaged White pupils in England that phrases such as "White privilege" and "toxic masculinity" were unhelpful. He said:

> *If we are now going to start teaching them in school that not only do they have to overcome the various economic and social barriers within their communities, but they also need to start apologising for belonging to a wider group which also strips away their individual agency, then I think we are going to compound many of these problems.*
>
> *My fear now is with the onset of new terms – toxic masculinity, White privilege – this is even actually going to become more of a problem as we send yet another signal to these communities that they are the problem.*

Then, in 2021, the Education Committee published a report, *The Forgotten: How White Working Class Pupils Have Been Let Down*,[1] saying White working-class pupils have been "badly let down by decades of neglect and muddled policy thinking".

So to blame "the White male" for all ills is incredibly unhelpful, incorrect and is why in my organisation, DIAL Global, we seek to work as one with allies, rather than demonising one particular group.

We are about inclusivity, and pointing out those who appear to have "had it easy", who've never "had to struggle" only plays into the hands of those who seek to spark division and rage.

Firstly, no one spends their time on this planet untouched by human pain. No matter what the external riches, being alive means some form of struggle at some point. Fear, grief, pain, illness, heartbreak, loss. There are some things that bank balances and fancy job titles can't protect you from. They may cushion the blow in some circumstances, but essentially no matter whichever socio-economic bracket one belongs to, we all weave in and out of other labels that can define us – perhaps for a short time. Perhaps forever.

Secondly, I strongly believe that there is enough success and opportunity to go around. I don't get filled with rage when I see another White man running a company. Instead I think, "Great. A potential ally. How can I meet this guy and talk to him about expanding the vision of his organisation and bring in opportunities for everyone?"

As the CEO of DIAL Global, I dedicate my life to bringing about real, tangible change. We're not out to demonise demographics who've benefited from the societal structure we find ourselves in. We're not the Robin Hood of the diversity world – seeking to take from the successful in order to give to the unheard.

We just want a workforce, indeed, a society, where everyone gets a chance. Where no matter what your ethnicity, social class, age, gender, sexuality or sexual identity, no matter what life has given you or robbed you of, you get a seat at the table.

You're heard.

Your face is in management, leadership, the C-suite, and the boardroom.

Your needs are understood in research and development (R&D) and people who look like you are represented in adverts.

If you have additional needs in the office, they're met without question or grumble.

You can show up as your whole self to work, to society in general, because you're valued.

I don't know about you but I was gripped by the Euros 2020 (which took place in the summer of 2021 due to the COVID-19 pandemic). I'm not normally a football fan, but to see those young lads, full of promise and talent, go so far in the competition warmed my heart immensely. I was moved enough to learn more about their backgrounds, and as I educated myself about the likes of Marcus Rashford and Raheem Stirling, reading about their humble backgrounds but endless dedication and skill, it reinforced to me the need for young people from underprivileged and minority ethnic backgrounds to be acknowledged, seen, amplified, and believed in. Rashford and Stirling, among others on that team, have an undeniable gift from God – but where would they be if not for the dedicated love, support, sacrifice and faith of mothers, sisters and those who spotted the talent and enabled the journey?

How many Stirlings and Rashfords are out there now, hidden in plain sight, because opportunity and support aren't in their orbit?

So let's extend that to the boardroom. Yes, there are CEOs who've risen from underprivileged and unexpected places to create something incredible – the rags-to-riches journey – but that's more often than not a space they've created themselves. Perhaps because they've had to?

In 2020, I was absolutely fascinated by research released by the National Federation of Self Employed and Small Businesses. They published a paper called *Unlocking* Opportunity,[2] which examined the minority ethnic-owned firms' contribution to UK enterprise and economies.

According to their data, ethnic minority businesses (EMBs) contributed £25 billion (BILLION!) to the UK economy in 2018, and "are more innovative and more likely to export than their non-EMB counterparts". But, the report also stated that many EMBs are held back by barriers which "hinder their growth" and "are often detached from mainstream business support, and struggle disproportionately when it comes to accessing finance".

And, in 2021, a report from think tank OPEN and MSDUK (a membership organisation working in the diversity space in supply chains) stated that "businesses led by ethnic-minority entrepreneurs contribute at least £74 billion a year" and "minority businesses make up 1/6 of the 6 million businesses registered in the UK and employed nearly 3 million people in 2019–20".[3]

I can't reiterate this enough. I'm not here to take away from the success that these hard-working and talented CEOs and C-Suiters have achieved. I'm not saying they had an unfair advantage. I'm not saying other people, given the chance, would do a better job.

I'm saying there's space for everyone. And I want to illustrate that by sharing my story, and my experiences. I've realised through time that sharing the pieces of my story does truly help other people.

I believe in intersectionality. I believe in the power of voices, and eclectic mixes – and I want to be able to use myself as the example.

I often feel so incredibly misunderstood, and I'm sure you have too. How many of us feel misunderstood, and different, and alone – so just conform to what is expected of us to save making a fuss or standing out even more than we feel we already do?

While there is a begging, crying, desperate need for us to think about the future generations of leaders and to support them – I truly believe there is a wider need for all of us, no matter what walk of life we come from, to rethink and reshape society.

Let's not conform to be cookie-cutter moulds, or stereotypes. Let's be conscious. Let's have conscious inclusion. I'm under no illusions that this is easier said than done, but I truly believe we can do this. My vision is crystal clear – the road to true diversity, equity, inclusion, belonging, and culture goes two ways.

One road heads in the direction of societal changes – what external factors need to be improved in our schools, workplaces, and communities to ensure that everyone in our world not just can exist in peace but also can thrive in their true selves, and how do we bring sceptics with us?

The other road leads inwards. What do we have to do as adult, self-aware, proactive, present members of the world in order to ensure we have our own innate sense of self, allowing us to step into our power, and claim our space with utmost confidence?

I must admit, my quest to truly find myself has been shaken hugely through the process of writing this book, as my beloved father died.

For anyone who is a member of this most unwelcome club, you will know what a seismic shift in our life losing a parent is.

I fell into a huge spiral of questioning my role in the world, my purpose in life, and what I want to have achieved by the time my own life comes to an end.

It's made me reflect so much on my past, my future, and what my dad always told me. "If you've done your best, darling, that's all that matters."

I've learned the long and hard way, but the journey was worth it. I hit rock bottom, I did the work to rise up, I found myself, my voice, and my space. And I've never been more inspired to help others do the same.

Notes

1. https://assets.publishing.service.gov.uk/media/616 ebbb1e90e071976488f8c/E02682727_CP_524.pdf
2. https://www.fsb.org.uk/resource-report/unlock.html
3. https://resources.msduk.org.uk/hubfs/Externally%20 Shared%20Files/Redirected%20Files%20from%20 Touchpoint/MSDUK-Impact-Report-2021.pdf

3

Finding My Inner Activist CEO

When you look back at the timeline of your life, often things fall into place when you see them from another perspective.

My role as a CEO and my calling to be a leader I've now realised were an inevitability. I was a little girl searching for where I belonged, and I became a young woman searching for where I belonged. I couldn't find that place, so I built it myself.

So how does an adopted, Hong Kong-born, Harrogate-raised, dyslexic woman become an Activist CEO? Believe me, had you asked specific of my teachers when I was at school, the answer might not have always been particularly positive! But, life is a rich tapestry of experiences, learning, and interactions, and my tapestry has shaped me in a way I couldn't possibly have envisaged.

Like the other Activist CEOs I will introduce you to in this book, my professional outlook has been profoundly affected by my personal experiences. Those experiences eventually sparked something within me that made me realise, after what felt like years in the wilderness, what my purpose in life is.

That's not to say that the purpose remains consistent. To go back to the kaleidoscope analogy, just as our identity can change, how we bring our talents into the world can as well. I've been driven to make the world a more equitable place in many different ways – recruitment consultant, executive search consultant, CEO, and as I now find myself looking at life in a different way since the debilitating grief of losing my father, I have been questioning my place in the world once more and finding excitement at the prospect of continuing to help others do well by doing good.

Beginnings

I spent the first ten months of my life in an orphanage.

Please don't feel sorry for me. I know it sounds like something out of a Dickens' novel as my late dad might have said but, honestly, I'm fine with it. I was adopted by the most amazing people who will always be my "real parents" and I'm luckier than a lot of people who are raised by the people who actually physically made them. My brother and I have had so much love. We've been so wanted. I am so lucky, happy, and grateful every day for that.

That said, I always knew I was different. Not in an exceptional, "I'm going to change the world" way (that came later!) but in a "looking round my classroom and realising nobody looks like me" way.

Growing up in North Yorkshire in the 1990s, funnily enough, there weren't a lot of Chinese children knocking around.

My story is unusual, and it's what's driven me to be a campaigner in the Diversity, Inclusion, Belonging, Equity, and Culture space.

I was born in Hong Kong on 1 May 1986 to two teenagers who put me up for adoption rather than attempt to forge a relationship and force parenthood before they were ready. And I'm writing this without an ounce of bitterness in my thoughts, I promise. I'm sporadically in touch with the biological father, and I've met my biological mother also. I'll tell you more about that as we go on, but please know I understand their decision and I feel so incredibly, incredibly, incredibly lucky that I have the parents who adopted me, and the family that I have. They're the reason that I do everything that I do every single day.

It's unlikely that I have any true memories from that time, but the stories I've been told have merged together in my fertile, active, youthful imagination, to create a faux image of my chubby-cheeked self as a baby, peering out from cot bars at prospective parents wondering if this would be the couple to take me home. I often think I remember this, though psychology would imply it's a memory I've created in my imagination. But I love to think I can remember the moment my family came into existence.

When I was ten months old, one of those couples *did* take me home. Ex-pats working in Hong Kong who'd never managed to have biological children of their own, having tried for over 10 years, their arms and hearts were open and ready to love this baby who looked nothing like them, but was theirs through and through. There's a photo I treasure of my parents holding me outside the court after getting the legal right to adopt me. It's such a gorgeous picture – me with my little fat pumpkin face, Mum looking like a true English rose with her curly dark brown hair and incredible height. My dad stands so proudly next to us both, over 6 foot, with a moustache and, as we joke, looking like John Cleese who plays Basil Fawlty in *Fawlty Towers*. It's such a powerful picture, I often wonder how my life might have panned out if they'd not come to the orphanage that day.

It's a photo which seems so simple at first glance, but demonstrates just how complex life can be and how our experiences shape us so much. The British couple living in a foreign land, dealing with what being "different" means. The husband and wife's private struggle to fall pregnant. The new parents smiling oh-so-proudly with their new daughter. This moment, life-changing for both me and them, doesn't just capture a new beginning but also a universal truth. We are not just the product of our DNA but the product of our upbringing, our rich experiences – good and bad – and ultimately we're multifaceted beings with so much richness of experience to offer the world if given the chance. Love is ubiquitous and it is nurture just as much as nature that shapes who we are.

My brother, also adopted, came along a few years later. He was born on Christmas Day so we still have a cutting of him from a Hong Kong magazine because he was a famous Chinese Christmas baby! Mum has created two books from when we were babies, everything from the adoption and our early years. They were created to help us understand the concept of adoption, and in order to navigate that understanding, we were encouraged to take part by decorating them ourselves.

I'd love to be able to go back to that time and watch it all unfold as an adult, knowing what I know now about the world. The first six years of my life, those formative years lived in a land so far away have left me with only vague, fuzzy memories – snatches of moments like flashbacks in a movie. As an adult now, I interpret these experiences in such a different way, and have spent an increasing amount of time wondering what it was like for my beautiful White parents to be raising a Chinese baby in Hong Kong.

But, of course, we can't do that, so all I have is the memories, the stories and the beginning of the rich tapestry that we make throughout our short time on this earth.

And my tapestry is made up of so many diverse, rich, colourful pieces of cloth – stitched together over time to create a story which on a challenging day is somewhat confusing, but on a good day fills me with nourishment and pride.

I'm often asked if I remember the moment I got told I was adopted, as if it was a hugely profound key part of my life. But the truth is, I don't. Apparently little Leila was quite nonchalant about the whole thing. People would look at us as a family, and ask the same questions over and over – and it became my "normal". I remember being in the playground one day and once again being asked what it felt like to be adopted, and just shrugging – baffled as to why I was always asked the banal question. I don't know how it feels to be adopted because I don't know how to feel any *other* way. Chinese people would come up to me and try to speak to me, and I wouldn't understand. Mum and Dad would then step in and explain, using the Chinese word for adopted. Retrospectively, I can't imagine how weird that would have been for them.

But our family made sense to us. Our life in Hong Kong made sense to us. I often think about families who are biologically related but are nothing more than four people living under the same roof. My family have no shared biology, no shared DNA, and we may have looked unorthodox to the outside world. But we were, and remain, a tight-knit family full of love and respect for each other. And honestly? Does a 4-year-old care about biology when she's fallen in the playground and wants her mummy to kiss it better? I can tell you from experience, no, she does not.

So there we were – two new parents living a wonderful life as ex-pats, with two much-longed-for and adored children. Yes, we were inundated with quizzical looks and a lot of questions, but we didn't know any different. And we were more than happy, we were filled with love for one another.

It was a life full of rich experiences and other cultures, and as I was lucky enough to go to an international school – I was never "different" back then. There's a really great picture I have from that time (which is probably very similar to every school picture you have as well) and I love it because the faces staring back at me are children of all different races and ethnicities. It was international, it was multicultural – and to me that was normal.

I was, of course, blessed to have parents who were actually very forward-thinking when it comes to breaking societal norms and forging their own path. You could, in fact, think of my parents as the original Activist CEOs in my life. It was my dad who actually followed my mum out to Hong Kong. She had the amazing job offer to work for the NHS. They built a great life out there, and lived a really wonderful, comfortable life, but they worked really, really damn hard for it.

But the time came when Mum and Dad felt it was time to head back to the UK – not an easy decision for them, and one I feel they've always grappled with. My mum did her best not to look back at a country much changed, and often said, "It was time to leave", but I know my dad found the decision hard, and his sadness more of a challenge to hide.

I, of course, was oblivious to what was happening as we prepared to say goodbye to Hong Kong – it was all one big adventure as I focused on where we were going, not what we were leaving behind. There was a little girl I was friends with, called Sarah, who was Irish with red hair and was absolutely gorgeous. She was my best friend, and I can still see her waving me off in the taxi with tears running down her face as I just beamed and waved, excited to get on a plane and see what would happen next.

Hong Kong to Harrogate

Our new life on Hills Road in Harrogate was quite literally a world away from the international bustle of Hong Kong.

Moving back to England was a culture shock for all of us. My parents had all the grown-up emotional fall-out to deal with, whereas my brother and I had to navigate a whole new world. New schools, new house, and of course – looking very, very Chinese in a notoriously middle-class White town.

We were super-lucky in every respect, though. We lived in a Victorian detached house, with a lovely back garden full of leafy trees and a climbing frame. I remember the big drive and fireplaces being so exciting after a lifetime spent in our very modern Hong Kong apartment.

We started a new primary school (though my earliest memory of that was clinging on to my mum, terrified, wondering what was about to happen) and seeing snow for the first time.

Home smelled like roast dinner, because my mum is a brilliant cook. Dad and I would argue over the best bits of the crackling on the pork, and we were an eclectic image of North Yorkshire respectability.

I came out of my first day of school holding the hand of another little girl called Thallia who was half-Chinese – obviously making a beeline for someone who resembled me, however slightly.

Yet, Hong Kong was never too far away wherever we looked. Maybe it was to keep my brother's and my heritage close to our hearts, or maybe it was for my parents to cling on to a time they loved so much, but either way – my childhood continued to be touched by my birthplace.

One of the highlights of the year once we were back in England, was visiting the Chinese supermarkets. It was such a special event – going into Leeds, heading to Chinatown and setting foot into a world that was so familiar and yet so alien.

I remember the unusual smells, the craziness, the hustle and bustle, the foreign tongue, and chitter chatter. It was overwhelmingly busy, with cramped little aisles you have to squeeze through to get past people.

We'd forage for almost all our sweets in there and it was a real treasure trove. The little chocolate panda biscuits I loved, the little lucky candy that came in red shiny foil packets (which went on to play a crucial role in my social life at primary school) and the little white chewy sweets called Lucky Rabbits. It wasn't all candy heaven though – there'd be mountains of Chinese vegetables with a not unpleasant but slightly earthy smell. The supermarkets were not necessarily always the cleanest-looking places in honesty, but definitely exciting.

I still get that same sense of excitement and anticipation when I go into the Chinese supermarket down the road from where I live now. I could spend hours foraging in the aisles looking for goodies and always end up coming out with bags overflowing with food and treats – I'm literally the kid in the candy store. I can't help myself – my heart flutters, and I'm overwhelmed with excitement. Paradoxically, I feel at home and yet like a complete foreigner at the same time.

Staff will see me, and start talking to me in Chinese. Then when they see my blank face and panicked expression, they'll realise I can't speak their language and you can see the confusion in their eyes.

It's a weird irony to realise that no matter where I am, I'm somehow always "different". There's a limit to how much that bothers me though – I've never had a victim mentality, and I'm very much a believer in making the most of whatever comes your way. One of the many, many things my parents did so right in raising us, was always emphasising and reiterating the positive side of Chinese culture. It wasn't just about sharing the culture with us, teaching us about it and making us understand the whys and wherefores. It was the active embracing and celebrating of it.

Chinese New Year was always a big event in our home, and it was where I would go on my best charm offensive at school. Let me explain. Every single Chinese New Year we would go for a Chinese meal with the family. It was amazing. And it was normal. And that was great.

Everyone would get together for incredible food at a restaurant in Leeds, and my dad would tell stories, they would reminisce and it would be brilliant to see him filled with joy, but a subtle reminder of how much he'd lost in leaving his spiritual home.

In Chinese culture, at New Year, people are given gifts (usually money) in little red Chinese pockets, almost like envelopes. The red symbolises luck, happiness, and energy and it's a huge part of the New Year tradition. We would put all of the lucky candies into the red pockets, take them in school, and then hand them out to everyone. I remember the buzz and the excitement, and the pride that I was the most popular person for that day.

I think about this tradition we made quite a lot. When you are, for whatever reason, in the minority of a group of people – do you hide what makes you different or do you embrace it, share it, and let others learn from your experiences? I'd argue the latter, but as we get older and more jaded by experiences and the world at large, perhaps we need to go back to the naïve innocence of our childhood. To the other kids that day, me sharing a huge part of Chinese culture wasn't symbolic or important – I just made people happy because I brought sweets.

Sometimes life is that simple.

Which is why it's imperative that we get inclusion right from the get-go. So much starts in school. Imagine if we started teaching kids about inclusion and belonging and the need to make people feel that they belong. Imagine what that would translate to in the workplace. No child is born racist, no child is born with bias. We're blank pages, sponges picking up on our environment.

And yet early on in our development, we start to absorb messages, either overtly from the words and actions of our caregivers and main influencers, or subliminally through things as seemingly innocent as our picture books and toys.

So much of the world around us has come into being by those who are simply creating something from their own experiences, their own life vision, their own lens. But we don't really look at how far-reaching this is until we know to look for it.

I don't know when was the last time you read a children's book, or perhaps visited the kids' section of a library, but next time you do, just take a moment to see how diverse and inclusive those stories are – and if youngsters in wheelchairs, or with neurodiversity, or of a minority race or faith see themselves represented in the pages of those books. Our concept of how relevant we are starts at an incredibly early age, so what message does it send to children if they don't see themselves in their own storybooks?

I hated dolls as a child. I loved dinosaurs, and anything with animals, but dolls made me cry. Someone bought me a doll once and I burst into tears. It's not a massive surprise really, I was a little girl and depictions of little girls in toys didn't resemble familiarity.

When did you ever see a Chinese doll or a black doll in the 1990s? I got excited if I saw one with brown hair. I'd say "that doll's got brown hair like me!"

I didn't see my face on dolls or on the TV, and it made me feel like I didn't matter. All I wanted was to be blonde and blue-eyed. That was all I wanted.

We become a product of our environment, and are shaped massively by external influences. So it's not just about teaching kids at home and at school to be kind – it's the toys they're looking at, the books that they're reading, and the images they're seeing on TV programmes and advertising.

One of the things I often wonder about life – especially through the lens of diversity and inclusion – is how much of our adult personalities are shaped by our early experiences and how much of us is already there from the moment we're born.

I look back at my formative years and wonder how much of my insecurities, my worries, and my anxieties were drawn from my experiences as a Chinese child in a White community, as a child struggling with dyslexia and as an adopted child – or how much it comes from me being an over-analytical and over-anxious little girl.

Now there's no question my ethnicity and my neuro-diversity impacted my childhood. While these experiences absolutely shaped me as a woman today, there is much of my young adulthood that was also very typical of all teenage girls growing up and figuring out who on earth we are.

My early years in Hong Kong provided me with a vibrant, international and nourishing start in life, and once ensconced in leafy Harrogate, my little primary school and all that went with it, I was safe in a bubble of almost mundanity. And that's no bad thing, by the way. If the worse thing you can say about your childhood was that it was safe, stable, and predictable, then you can definitely count yourself lucky. Sports days, nativity plays, play dates, and playmates – my little life was as secure as I could hope for.

It was later on that I realised we were living in a bubble. As my world expanded and I hit secondary school age, I met a different group of people. The types of people you meet as you say goodbye to hopscotch, coat pegs with your name on and little glasses to fit your tiny hands.

As you go out into the big bad world of high school, you realise that kids move around in packs. We have labels on our foreheads and it's hard, if not impossible, to move between stereotypes.

If my parents were early adopters of inclusivity training, the social structure of teenagers is a masterclass of how not to do inclusion. We spoke earlier about the dangers of individuals having their identity defined by a simple box, rather than fluid kaleidoscopes, and that's never better demonstrated than by our teenage experiences! Once you have one identity that's it – unless you're extremely lucky, there's little chance of veering in and out of the boxes in which we find ourselves.

You don't need to be a psychologist to know why it's so crucial at that age, as we are learning about ourselves and learning about the world in which we're starting to navigate as adults, that we need clear signposts to allow us to identify ourselves and those people shaping our world.

But when you're not the one in charge of doing the hat sorting, then waiting to see which groups will accept you is a daunting thing.

My main problem in my teenage years was worrying about what everyone thought of me all of the time. Entirely normal for any teenager, and yet doubly hard when you feel so very different.

I was definitely not in a group. I was always on the periphery. A loner. I could manage to blend in with most people and I don't think I was massively disliked by anyone. I would just kind of bubble around – an observer, moving between groups quite easily. I liked that I didn't have to commit to one personality type.

I was really good at art, and I adored the teacher as it felt to me it was the only subject in which I got taken seriously. I loved the unleashing of creativity, and my teacher saw that in me. She was encouraging, she was complimentary, and I belonged. I remember thinking it was like she could tell I felt I was a little bit different.

Like most teenagers, I went through a bit of a rebellion, yet looking back through the kinder eyes of a more experienced adult I would perhaps now "re-brand" that rebellion as simply trying out different identities until I found one that fit. I was a bit of a rock kid for a while, then trying different looks, different hairstyles, different fashions. Which external persona suited the confusion within me?

My art teacher seemed to be the only person who noticed these phases, my mini-identities, which was another reason why I really liked her! Most people just want to be seen. To be acknowledged in this big, loud, overwhelming world.

My psychology teacher was amazing because she was so damn passionate about what she did. Ironically, I actually hated psychology, and I remember going to her to try and quit. I ended up doing it for A Level – so that says a lot about the power of an open mind.

Neither woman made me feel silly. Both made me feel like I had a voice, and like I had some kind of significance in what was the pretty ferocious world of school both provided me with the psychologically safe environment in which I look back on and realised I craved. They were key fixtures in a scary environment who made the art of inclusion and belonging seem effortless.

Once we get past a certain age, the markers that seem so important at the time start to fade. We're no longer asked which GCSEs we're doing or what A Levels we got. It all fades away into another jigsaw piece of our past. But my A Levels, I feel, were so key to my life because they fundamentally still represent who I am today – art, psychology, and business. My physical identity may have changed, but my internal one clearly hasn't!

Much of my teen years were probably very familiar to every other teen going through adolescence. Who am I and where do I fit in? But there was one part of that puzzle I felt I couldn't answer, and, at 17, I was desperate to.

I didn't know anything about the couple who brought me into this world.

I may have been part of an idyllic picture book family, but I didn't look like them – and while my parents always were and always will be the people I truly consider my mum and dad, in my tumultuous teenage years I felt like I needed to grab onto something from my past in the vain hope it would help me understand my present and navigate my future.

So I did something I've regretted to this day.

I went to find my birth parents.

Searching for Something

While it was 20 years ago, and I should reflect on that period with kindness towards my young and confused self, I still find it excruciatingly painful to relive. I get a knot in my stomach and a weight in my chest when I consider what it must have done to my mum and dad. Their once adorable little baby, into whom they'd poured all their love and hopes, was staring back at them in rage and asking for a refund. It is one of the greatest regrets of my life and if I could undo it, I would.

The rebellious phase was well underway. Coloured strips in my hair. Pierced tongue. Pierced nose. I sat down with my mum and dad and told them I wanted to find my birth parents. God knows what they must have thought, but, as ever, they were amazing.

They said "no problem", and within a week, dad had got in touch with the adoption agency and found my birth mother, who – it turned out – was happy to meet me. My darling beloved dad organised it all.

I flew out to Hong Kong with my then boyfriend ready to face the missing piece of my identity. Once I was in the room with the woman from whom I came, I knew my Chinese self would make sense and everything would fall into place. I wouldn't be different any more – I'd make sense.

I left five minutes later in tears.

I had to get out of that room as quickly as physically possible because this woman did not resemble anything to do with me or my life.

I was already struggling with being different. I'd already absorbed so many messages from the world around me that Chinese meant "not beautiful" and I'd spent years perfecting my make-up to ensure my eyes looked more Western. So many small things had happened to me over the years that I'd built up a picture of my identity which was fragile when it came to my relevance and beauty in the eyes of the rest of the world.

I was faced with a woman I couldn't relate to, a stereotype of a country I barely knew – which in my young mind reinforced my own fears I was "less than". I think I've had a complex about it over the years. I've never wanted to look like what I am.

You perhaps think that me running away from my birth mother in tears may have been the weirdest thing to happen that day. It wasn't. Far from it. Once I'd recovered from the emotion of the experience, we headed to a nearby shopping centre for lunch – and bumped into her almost immediately. It was hugely awkward but I decided I had to take the plunge and we had lunch together. Her English was broken and our conversation limited.

Over the trip I met her a couple of times, and even met my birth grandmother, and my half-brother.

But that's not all.

A few days after my initial meeting with my birth mother, the phone in the hotel room began to ring. I answered, slightly surprised, and the unfamiliar voice on the other end dropped a bombshell. "Oh, hello. This is your birth father's wife."

The woman on the other end of the phone was married to the man who'd got my birth mother pregnant and had somehow tracked me down. I'd not gone to try and find my birth father, but news of my arrival must have come through the Chinese network.

She told me she was going to come to the hotel to meet me and it would take two hours for them to get there.

You can imagine my reaction.

Eventually a bright blue Subaru Impreza turns up and out gets a small Chinese man in a three-piece suit who says, "Hi, I'm Patrick. Your birth father."

We sat and talked and ironically he'd lived in the UK for years, near Manchester. Contact with my birth parents didn't end there. There were flurries of birthday presents, both came to see me in the UK when I was younger, and I hear from them occasionally.

Meeting them didn't give me the answers that I thought I would get, and at times even raised more questions for me.

However, they are certainly jigsaw pieces that I've been able to put into the correct place.

But that didn't mean I was any happier within my identity. I was still lost.

Coming of Age

I've spoken so much about my parents in the book so far, which isn't a huge surprise as I think subconsciously this is almost a love letter to them. A thank you letter for finding me, choosing me, loving me, accepting me, and forgiving me – forgiving me for teenage blips and for adult disasters.

My mum and dad never really asked much of me or my brother Michael, but the one thing they never made a secret of was that they wanted us to go to university. I think that was a sign that they'd really given us every chance, and it was the icing on the cake of a happy, safe, and secure childhood.

I'd had conflicting thoughts this, unsure if it was for me. I had a teacher at school who told me I was an interesting juxtaposition between being rebellious and studious simultaneously. I've always been black and white, night and day. I've never been in the middle ground – which you're about to realise.

My love of art led me to doing an Art Foundation course in Leeds, before heading off to Manchester to do a business degree. If you've made a huge change in your life, then you'll know how scary it can be. The world seemed a bigger place because I became a master of my own destiny.

For the first year, I didn't fit in with anyone. That's an irony not lost on me, because years after attending my beloved international school in Hong Kong I once again found myself in a truly multicultural environment – and I didn't fit in at all. I didn't identify with the Chinese students I was meeting as they sat at the back of lectures with translators, and I continued to fail to find my tribe.

Then, as now, I found salvation in work. I'd had a job since I was 15 as I yearned to earn money, develop my skills, and be an active part of society. I always felt more comfortable in a working environment than I did in an educational one. So while everyone else was smoking pot in university, I put signs up on all of the other dorms saying that I could do people's nails for £20. I worked in coffee shops, restaurants, clubs, and bars and was even a shot girl for a while as well – always on the hustle and being entrepreneurial and saving my money to eventually buy my first house.

But after a year in Manchester, not finding my feet and missing a boyfriend back in Leeds – I left university to be closer to home and complete my degree at Leeds Metropolitan University. I suppose it was predictable – I didn't find my tribe there, I didn't feel I belonged and I had divided my attention by spending so much time working.

I came out of university having somehow achieved a first Class Honours Degree and the highest mark in my graduating year. Yet, somehow, I could not secure myself a job. My CV got me through all the doors I could ask for, and each interview was an adventure – walking through the doors of many shiny corporate offices where I longed for a graduate programme that would allow me to cut my teeth in the world of work. Despite my efforts, I did not receive one single job offer and so I continued to work and to hustle, all the while fearing that I simply must not be "good enough".

Having just bought my first house at the age of 21, I got into the world of TV extras, promotional work, and events and generally working as much as I possibly could in order to get my feet onto the property ladder. I didn't make great choices during this period, and I know my parents worried about me. I didn't care then though. I was just happy I finally had good friends. I was accepted I was in charge of my own destiny or so I thought. Clearly now I see that this was a mirage – a desperate young woman, lost away from the security of home, unsure as to who she was, and who she was supposed to be.

I was searching for something, and what I'd failed to find in my identity, I found in misfits and friends – and a club owner who was, surprise, surprise . . . Chinese. I became close to him, on a friendship level and nothing more, but I liked him and felt comfortable with him.

I found myself wanting to please him and looking up to what he had achieved in his many business ventures.

It was so utterly predicably and transparent looking back. But that's where I was. Attracted to a world where looks were important and being different was OK. I was accepted by all around me I felt and mentored by someone with my heritage.

Yet it truly was my rock bottom.

It's my "dark years", the period that makes me cringe, that sums up just how deeply affecting never belonging can be. I have been so hard on myself about that time for so very long. It's only as I've got older I have realised I was a lost child, and gave myself permission to forgive her.

Starting Again

After I'd hit rock bottom, and took solace in the arms of my parents, I began to build myself back up.

I knew work would be my salvation (and also my dad told me I had to get a proper, stable job!!), so after thinking about my strengths and taking some sound counsel, I began working in recruitment. The drive, the adrenaline, the targets, and the meritocracy proved an enticing mix for me – and I was really, really good at it. I can't say I loved all the companies I worked with – there was a level of pretension with one which I struggled with, and I feared becoming a cliché. But I worked hard, kept my head down, and soon saw the rewards.

It wasn't long before I took the plunge and set up on my own – with a new outlook on life and ready to make my mark.

I bought my second home, a little two-up, two-down, and set up Loft Talent Acquisition in my front room. I had one member of staff, and then started hiring apprentices. Before long I moved into an office opposite Canal Street in Manchester – onto the top floor because it was the absolute cheapest. The lift always smelled of marijuana and there were holes in the walls of the office and even though the business was growing, I never thought I had it all nailed – inside I've always been scared. I'd run downstairs to find a little crevice next to the bins, I'd go and smoke and basically call a guy I paid a grand a month to be a mentor, an unofficial Non-Exec Director. But I kept working hard, building the business and as it grew and grew I took a huge leap. I quit the office on Canal Street and moved into a really swanky office in King Street where we employed multiple people. But soon we had £35,000 a month in overheads and the pressure to maintain it was huge.

At this point I met my now husband, Costa Delis, who saw my vision through new eyes and helped me scale back to start again. I took that experience to Leila McKenzie Associates, a boutique executive search firm specialising in niche hires. We made some huge hires and some great fees, I was at the peak of my career – but something was missing.

I just thought there was so much more I could do to make a difference.

I asked myself how much change I was really making in recruitment. So many hires seemed to be a battle, and I was seeing so much talent waiting in the wings but with nowhere to go. I knew the whole system needed a shake-up, and over time I realised my network could be the way to do that.

I was surrounded by great leaders and inspiring contacts. I wanted to use them to inspire and educate and motivate others to make the world a better place.

After many sleepless nights and random voicemails full of ideas left on other people's phones, I finally realised the direction I would take. I started a podcast called Diverse and Inclusive Leaders with individuals who I was drawn to due to their interesting and unique backgrounds and those that I had met along my way through the world of executive search, often previous clients or candidates. The initial concept was Dial mentors (we should all have one or many!). It was my friend Simon Tyler, an executive coach who suggested the name "Dial" as he could see that I was trying to move the dial in the right direction. From here, Dial Global was born. It stands for "Diverse, Inclusive, Aspirational Leaders".

I'm immensely proud of DIAL Global, and I'm driving as hard as I can for upward social mobility across multiple intersectional lenses of diversity, inclusion, belonging, equity, and culture.

4

Fill Up Your "S" Cup

Life is all about teamwork. Whether it's in a marriage, friendship, NCT group, or the boardroom, we all have to embrace our differences and find a way to work together for an end, a shared goal.

Sometimes it takes work to find that chemistry, and sometimes fate intervenes.

In 2022, I was lucky enough to take part in a six-week intensive course at the University of Cambridge, called the Wealth Economy. It's a framework for sustainable prosperity beyond GDP. In simple terms, we count wealth in monetary terms, like pounds and dollars. But, actually, wealth is many other things. It's knowledge capital. It's human capital. It's social capital. It's natural capital. How do we measure that? It's far more difficult as it is classed as intangible.

My tutor for this course, Dr Sangaralingam Ramesh, introduced me to Dr Adel Dalal, who at the time was a Postgraduate Teaching Assistant at UCL. Adel got her PhD in Russia (Higher School of Economics) and has a background in sustainable finance, supervising students' research at UCL and HSE, and being a member of CFA UK Society, she's currently obtaining a certificate in ESG investing.

The creative connection we made really hammered home to me that in life, sometimes you have these weird chance meetings. You don't always know why you will end up taking the certain life path that you do, but often they end up leading you to meet with the people who can have a real impact on your life. They teach you new things, they make you think differently. And let's face it, life is not a rose petal-strewn path of wonder. It's littered with challenges. It's littered with hurdles that we kind of try and get over and try and come out the other end somehow a better person.

I was so impressed by her and her colleague Dr Sangaralingam Ramesh, that I commissioned them to do some research into my vision to measure the importance of the social pillar, the "S" in ESG (Environmental, Social, and Governance), creating the foundations for an "S Framework" for DIAL as an evolution on from our 10 dial diversity facets, which will eventually allow us to monitor and measure the ever-increasing importance of organisations and their ethical credentials. Adel was immediately keen to work on our DIAL's latest venture and found that every one of the measurement standards that we could find for the S in ESG had Diversity, Inclusion, Belonging, Equity, and Culture within it in one guise or another. Adel was as passionate as I was about this opportunity. She said, "I think it is important because it is one of the first attempts to make a rating which is also industry agnostic, which is very different from current standard ratings of the S in ESG, and it's also size agnostic, which is important because we're not focusing solely on large companies. We also want to give an instrument to mid-size enterprises to also have their voice and have their social efforts be heard and be assessed."

I wanted to sit down with Adel for this book to delve deeper into this and found out that, like all of us, she was driven by personal experience.

Adel is based in Russia, so we booked in some time to sit down on a video call, and I asked her about her inner Activist CEO:

Diversity has always been a very personal issue to me. I'm half-Indian, half-Russian and I was born in Kazakhstan. Part of my childhood I spent in Argentina before we moved to Russia. So "feeling foreign" was a normal thing. Just not fitting in. It's like a blessing in one way because you always stand out, there's more attention. For example, my name.

Because in Russia it's not a common name, and people also have middle names that come from their father's name. And because my father is Indian, I didn't have that, so I sometimes couldn't even book tickets like flights just because I couldn't tick this box. So that's how absurd lack of diversity could be.

I can't complain, never complained, I'd never been bullied, I would say, but it's just like this internal, this inner feeling that you are different in some way or another, which again is a good thing, but sometimes you feel lonely, obviously.

Throughout my journey I had this first encounter with diversity in a very personal way. Then I saw the lack of diversity that affected directly my career path and now obviously I have a different twist on it because, again, if you live in another country, you think that you have a completely international background and you spend so much time studying abroad and you have so many friends, but still, there are some traits that you didn't know you had them until you just try to integrate into a new community.

Despite Adel's academic approach to inclusion and ESG in business, she is focused on, as I am, hope.

She said:

I'm very happy I met you and I always enjoy talking to you because you need to believe that we can make the world a better place. No matter how pretentious, how hyped this statement is, you have to believe in it. Otherwise why? What is the purpose of waking up in the morning? I don't know. I'm from the financial industry, where people like to make jokes about ESG and sustainability, so it's nice to actually build a community of people who believe that we can change something. And it's not just that it's just because we want to because it's cool to be sustainable, diverse, but because otherwise we would all go to hell.

I found Adel's words really moving – and was particularly connected to something which has always resonated with me. The fear of being a victim. As I said to her in our conversation, "You're a glass half-full person. I can tell that you've got fire in your belly when you speak the words of the fact that you are lucky, and you feel lucky. I do the same thing. I'm not a victim. I feel lucky I was adopted. I feel lucky that this has happened. I feel blessed that the diversity and the richness of the family have given what it's given me. And in the same way having an Indian father and a Russian mother has given you this unique view on life and view on the world."

We spoke about the importance of keeping a positive world view, when working on our inner activist. I pointed out to Adel that while we know humans can be amazing, they can also be the biggest accelerators to perpetuating negative beliefs.

I had scrawled in my notebook as I listened to Adel speak, "ESG . . .. positive belief like a new religion?" as it occurred to me the people need to have that feeling of belief, that gives them that feeling of belonging, that gives them the foresight and almost like the vision to know that there are better things ahead, despite the controversy, despite the negativity.

Adel agreed, adding,

> It's a very good point because religion actually drives us to a better future, to heaven. I would be happy if ESG would be a new religion now. And I also am very happy about the changes or just the conversations that are happening right now that we already are, obviously not as much as we would want to, but at least we are moving so we're going somewhere.
>
> But when I look back at my journey and what made me stoic about my values and what I want to do, is that I believe you need to wake up in the morning and not just hate your life, basically. Or just waiting for your annual bonus to pay for your therapy just because you can't feel without it. Or just trying to fulfil yourself with other material stuff just to feel happier.
>
> But also what played a huge role in my current standing is mentorship. And it's not like this very formal coaching. These are just people

that you come across and they completely change your life. They have no idea they did it. It's just because who they are and what energy they bring to the world.

Adel expanded on this point by reminding us that when we talk about Activist CEOs, we shouldn't just focus on those running organisations and fulfilling the stereotypical leader profile. She referred to her mentor in academia:

It's just absolutely the energy he puts into his students. You see that he lights up just from thinking about issues, and his energy. And he cared about me more than many people that were much closer to me, just because of who he is. He could send me on LinkedIn at midnight, some job, some new position and I feel like, "Okay, that's who I want to be when I grow up." And that's what drives you, actually.

That's why we're talking about how important it is to be the Activist CEO, to actually champion responsible leadership, sustainable leadership, because, again, it's a huge responsibility. You can change people's lives in so many ways, not knowing about it.

And I feel this effect with my tutor. He is my senior. He's a very distinguished professor and scholar. And he is, in some way, that CEO that actually affected my career and my choices.

I added:

He's your Activist CEO. He sounds fascinating. And I can feel you being excited because of the energy that he's given you. It's the passing on of knowledge and care and empathy and thought beyond yourself where he saw something. It's that belief. He has the belief in you. And you referenced there, almost more belief than some people that you've known for a long time.

We talk of "real models" and "role models", and I like to talk of them as "real models" because they aren't necessarily some archetypal stereotype of what a role model for a girl would have been 20 years ago. But actually it's someone who's smart, who cares, who has capability to make us feel like you belong and can teach you something. These real models are, without knowing, sharing their knowledge, sharing their wisdom, imparting some positive energy on you and having that belief.

I think it's interesting that all throughout the conversation we've had, we keep circling back to the belief, and to the belonging. The belief and the belonging and the will to succeed. Something beyond yourself almost?

Adel agrees, telling me about her professor's gruelling sporting regime, and points out that energy comes from love.

You need to love what you do and he cares so much about what he does and for that reason he wants to nurture a new generation to help him do what he's doing. And if you don't love what you do, then you don't want other people to succeed. Because if it becomes so hard that every morning you have to put a mask on, then you would think, "Okay, why should others have it any other way? If I had to earn it the hard way, why would I want my buddies to have it an easy way?"

It's almost like being jealous about junior people. There is research proven that the main facilitator of sustainable leadership is experience of sustainable leadership. So if you were raised with these mentors, obviously you want to put it through yourself and your own experience to your juniors.

Then when you grow further in your career and when you had it very hard, many of us cannot break through it and become bitter, and don't understand how to then love other people. And it's very hard to change this routine.

I'm struck again by the parallel with religion, as I told Adel.

It's super-profound. It sounds really quite religious because what you're saying is we have to love others, we have to love ourselves. We have to also be able to forgive because it's easy to become quite bitter.

I almost sense at times I can feel anger when I feel like people don't believe you, or you have to fight quite hard for something. And I think if that was accentuated further, you can find yourself in almost a perpetual cycle of despair, a perpetual cycle of feelings of jealousy or envy or some of the things that no one willingly wants to have as traits.

Which is why it's so important to continue to give and send a lift back down. And we're thinking about what we want to be when we grow up, and the idols that we have are those that are giving.

My dad always wanted the best for me. Your parents wanted the best for you and they push you to succeed with their definition of success. So you can look after yourself and give you the tools like this. Your professor has to help you in the next stages of your career. And that's something to be commended because we're in a world which can be quite transactional at times.

You can't judge people necessarily by your own standards and so, ultimately, what do you do? Do you hate or do you choose love? Do you choose forgiveness? Do you, as you very profoundly said, try and break the cycle because what else do you do? You have to break the cycle or you end up becoming one of those people.

We've all seen them, where you think "Oh, my goodness, they have the sense that the world is against them. They don't want other people to succeed." Jealousy, envy can be some of the most challenging and horrible things and so lifting oneself out of those is having role models and real models to be able to look to.

Adel then drew the conversation back to the all-important concept of the S in ESG.

It's very hard to be this ethical, responsible, sustainable CEO. Obviously resources are scarce and we need to allocate them as efficiently as possible and people are fighting for these resources. But I think we need to change our understanding of what "resource" is because for now, in the ESG discussion, currently, I feel that today, still it is juxtaposed. Even in reporting, we have financial reporting and then we have non-financial reporting.

Now there is more evidence that actually non-financial facilitates and positively affects financial. But still these are two things that we think, "Okay, I can be all ethical and moral, but then I will lose some of the other benefits." However, I feel that it should be treated differently.

There is even a framework, it's called Triple Bottom Line. It was developed by Elkinton and Rollins in the 1990s. So rather than focusing on the financial "bottom line", organisations should commit to measuring environmental, social, and financial factors. They're not juxtaposed.

I think we need to change our thinking fundamentally. I like that the discussion is moving towards what GDP is, because if we talk about sustainability but then the main factor of economic growth is consumption. These are two things that don't go together – so consume more or sustainability, right? So that means there's nothing wrong with sustainability, there's nothing wrong with responsible leadership. Maybe there's something wrong with the tools that we're just using these days.

I found this fascinating as it allowed me to articulate something which I have an ongoing issue with.

When you add a "non-" to start with at the beginning, it already feels less than. You're non-white. Okay, so you're not the pinnacle. Oh, you're not financial. You're non-financial. So you're not as good as the narrative frame. It's like there is a default option and then there is a switch.

The roads point to S being the most important. The S and the wealth economy framework are all around. Like knowledge capital, human capital, social capital, the sharing of networks. It's stuff that is intangible yet also it's obviously harder to measure. Are the S and the sharing of intangible resources the answer to our future world problems? I think that's so interesting.

Before I had to let Adel get back to work, she touched once again on consumption versus sustainability. "We just have to change our views in that way. The thing about consumption is sometimes we just put on a patch. It's like taking a pill to get rid of a symptom when we buy a new piece of clothing. But often it's just because we're drained so we're out of our resources. For that reason, again, it should be a bit redefined, I think. We need to fill up our S cup."

5

Addressing Behaviour Not Belief

The link between religion and diversity played on my mind after my interview with Adel. I found it ironic that faith in the work that we do, faith in our goal, faith we will achieve, and faith in our co-workers are so inherent to what we do, and yet, in my experience working with CEOs and organisations, there is always such reticence when approaching the issue of religion in the workplace.

We know that best practice in the field of DIBEC means starting a conversation that we know could be challenging, but we start the conversation, nonetheless. Whether we're talking about race, gender, disability, or sexuality – we know these are big areas that most people are scared to broach for fear of saying the wrong thing or causing offence. We still find it easier to explore all our other facets than we do religion.

Now, in some ways, we are pushing on an open door. Religion and belief discrimination is illegal in the UK and is listed as a protected characteristic in the Equality Act 2010.

In our 2023 DIAL Global review, we were reassured to see 94% of respondents stated that companies allowed them to take time off for religious holidays and holy days. Some 90% told us they were allowed to wear religious symbols and clothing, with 88% of respondents telling us free discussions about religion and belief were permitted in the workplace.

Some 84% of surveyed companies say they cater to different dietary requirements (up from 65% in 2022) and 82% say they provide a dedicated prayer space (up from 69% in 2022). And 74% of participating UK companies say they take specific steps to ensure managers are aware of their staff's religious needs (up from 53% in 2022). Data on religion is collected less often than some other facets of diversity, with 39% saying they do not collect any of this data.

In fact, the facet of religion was ranked second overall behind mental health.

Zareena Brown, Chief People Officer at Royal Mail, told us:

> *We know that having a religion or a belief system can offer a sense of comfort, purpose, and connection to others and that it influences the way we perceive the world around us.*
>
> *Faith and belief are deeply personal and meaningful aspects of individuals' lives and identities, influencing their values and perspectives on the world. Recognising and appreciating the rich tapestry of faith and religious diversity not only enhance our understanding of different cultures but also enrich personal and professional experiences, enabling colleagues to bring their full selves to work.*
>
> *Our vision at Royal Mail is to create an inclusive, accessible, and equitable culture, one that nurtures connection and belonging for all our people. We recognise the importance of religious beliefs to our colleagues, and highlight various religious events, raising awareness on the importance of these key dates across the organisation. We are passionate about creating safe spaces for our colleagues to carry out religious activities, to ensure all colleagues, regardless of their religion and belief system, feel included.*

In the US, it's also a fairly positive picture, with near-universal agreement that companies allow respondents to take time off for religious holidays and holy days (89%), allow employees to wear religious symbols and clothing (87%), and allow free discussions about religion and belief in the workplace (88%). This year, some companies are starting to track the religions or belief systems of their employees (23%, up from 0% in 2022).

Some 71% say they provide a dedicated prayer space and 54% of surveyed companies say they cater to different dietary requirements. And 57% of participating US companies say they take specific steps to ensure managers are aware of their staff's religious needs (up from 43% in 2022).

Data on religion is collected less often than some other facets of diversity, with 68% saying they do not collect any of this data. Overall in the US, religion ranked sixth in the diversity listing.

Reverend Mark Fowler is the CEO of the Tanenbaum Center for Interreligious Understanding. He stated:

> *Companies must be equipped with the knowledge and competencies necessary to attract and retain top talent. This includes recognising and understanding religion and belief as a facet of identity. It is important to recognise that religion is already present in each and every workplace. Implementing policies and practices that are inclusive of diverse religious practices and observations is therefore a requisite step for any company aspiring to lead in the diversity space.*
>
> *Diversity exists both across and within religious traditions. And the needs of diverse employees will look different both across industries and within organisations. There are no one-size-fits-all solutions, as employee needs are often context-specific and reflective of job function.*
>
> *That is why Tanenbaum promotes policies and practices that support employees of all faiths and none. Such an approach is a recognition of our intersecting identities and the opportunity to support all employees, regardless of how they identify.*
>
> *Failing to understand religion and belief in the workplace not only leaves companies ill-equipped to support their employees, but also vulnerable to the changing socio-political dynamics of our time. That is why it is so encouraging to have the DIAL Diversity Review as a resource. It is more critical than ever to reflect on our past, understand our current landscape, and make informed decisions about how to move the DIAL forward.*

Several times a year, we host the DIAL Global Summit where we run virtual and in-person panels to discuss best practice in the diversity arena, and look at future trends we may be dealing with down the line.

One of the stand-out sessions we've done on religion will always stay with me, as we brought together Reverend

Mark Fowler with Kathryn Wright, the CEO of Culham St. Gabriel's Trust, and Elly Tomlins, Chief People Officer at Britvic PLC. We discussed how a mutual respect of faith (or lack of) in the workplace was essential for inclusivity.

Mark explained from the outset that balancing religion and interpersonal relationships can be a challenge. "While many companies do allow open conversations on religion and appreciate the diversity this brings, it can also create tension, especially when religious or non-religious beliefs clash. How can you avoid conflict by encouraging employees to be open about their faith and associated values, but setting clear guidelines on what constitutes a professional business conduct at the same time?"

Kathryn stressed that while people can feel tensions around issues of faith, it's actually a very inclusive element of life. "We all have a position, whether it be religious or not. And we might say 'nobody stands nowhere'."

She continued:

I see the world through a lens which can be rooted in my culture, like upbringing, contextual factors, as well as religion or belief. And our world view can be complex, perhaps a mix of religion and non-religion. And my world view is bound up with my identity. This dimension impacts us all and is therefore about valuing, valuing our employees, our customers, our clients and so on.

Secondly, it's also important because a survey we commissioned found that two-thirds of the UK adult respondents said it's important to understand the beliefs of others, particularly in the workplace, and also around two-thirds thought that understanding their own beliefs was important to them, as well.

Over half agreed that understanding had a positive impact on their well-being. So it isn't just about understanding, it's about identity. It's about understanding who we are as people, which then impacts on how we live our lives and our sense of community and well-being with others. So, religion or belief, if it's important to 30 people, we really should be taking it seriously.

I really believe that so strongly, and I think if we understand this dimension, then actually it begins with all of us. And it begins with our own self-awareness. Being aware that we have a position and that we view the world through that position. And I think if we do that, that actually brings us to a place of humility, perhaps also a place of vulnerability as well.

It takes us to a place of listening. And I think listening is really, really key. I don't think we do enough, and I think it's one of the most important places to start with all of this. If we're listening, and actually we can begin to empathise, and we automatically take that place of humility with others.

I like the idea of being generous with our space – our intellectual space as well. Being open and generous in our space towards other people, and I think empathy and humility are part of that.

Elly told us:

We're living in an increasingly multicultural world, and, on top of that, we're also living in an increasingly polarised world. The advent of social media, the tone of voice that you hear online is getting increasingly shrill and increasingly intolerant.

Having active advocates for tolerance as it builds respect, as it builds empathy, as it builds humility, is so important because it's the force that gives me hope when I look into a world that is becoming more polarised and allowing highly political views to get charged against highly religious ones.

I think when you lean into empathy, when you lean into respect, when you lean into humility, it's much harder to maintain that kind of fixed perspective because you're listening. If you take the stance of listening and openness and self-awareness, the society you live in becomes more tolerant, becomes more open and you create space for people.

I think often people are not generous with their space. They live in a world that's online and they get offended quite quickly. A former colleague of mine once gave me a great phrase – "offence can be taken, it's rarely given". Empathy and humility always remind you to think from the other person's perspective and not take offence when you don't need to. And so I think it's a hugely valuable set of traits and set of leadership stances.

Reverend Mark added to this:

One of the things I'm always mindful of is that when we talk about empathy, as a behaviour, the foundation of it is actually listening. It is the deepest kind of listening, moving, engaged, that suspends our own beliefs and suspends our own feelings to actually really receive not just what someone is saying, but all the emotions. So I think it's wonderful that we're talking about empathy and respect rather than kind of theological concepts and things.

One thing that the CEOs I've spoken to for this book, or through the course of my work, have consistently told me is that Employee Resource Groups / Business Resource Groups or Networks are a crucial factor in the development of an organisation. And Kathryn agrees:

Networks are, I think, most effective when they are interfaith, or when religious and non-religious beliefs can be represented through them. Also being celebratory of your networks is key. I think sometimes there can be a focus on dealing with issues or challenges or problems. But, actually, what really struck me is the strength of the relationships between people. I think that's really powerful. Because I think if you build those relationships between people who have different world views, then actually when there are challenges, people will find it easier to go back to listening, so people will find it easier to listen to one another. I think sometimes there's a danger they're used for problem solving and not celebrating.

Elly built on this, talking about how Britvic build on raising awareness of their work.

Like every business, we're using a wide range of mechanisms to try and increase awareness and try and reach people. We're a relatively small business of about 4000 people globally. And therefore getting people involved and getting the voice of people who have lived experience in a given area is so crucial to engaging and building awareness.

We have a wide variety of things like TED Talks and books and podcasts and reports, as well as learning modules on everything from Windrush through to Black History Month. The other thing we've done, and it has been really lovely over the last 12 months, is hosting regular events to mark religious holidays and cultural celebrations. Hannukah, Christmas, Chinese New Year, Divali, Eid, Ramadan. The network team produced celebration boxes, to send to all our factories and offices across both Britain and Ireland, with chocolates and balloons, and it just made it visible and recognisable and had a lovely, lovely splash event, as well as that sense of generosity, that sense of celebration.

We've also done work to create that safe space to pray. I think that's really, really important.

I kind of came up with five areas or principles that I thought were probably quite important. My first one is to lean into the celebratory. It's so valuable to take those moments to celebrate what other people are celebrating, to ask people to walk a mile in each other's shoes and really understand what's valuable about their cultural heritage as well as their religion.

The second one I think is really important – don't shy away from being a little directive when you need to be. Don't say "you must be so hungry" to someone who is fasting. Find a way of asking interesting questions, without judgement, and using that curiosity to build and actually giving people permission to be honest – it's interesting and it builds connection by kind of creating those moments.

The last area is what do you do when you hit a boundary? Where this gets tricky is where one set of beliefs crashes into another set of beliefs. In other roles, we've had moments where we've gone out with policies for LGBTQIA+ and had groups who are more of a sort of fundamentalist Christian belief set, stand up and say, "I don't agree with this." As an HR person, and as a leader, it's in those moments where this stuff becomes really tricky. So it's really important to help your leaders find the boundaries that are meaningful to them.

I found this point particularly resonated with me. When we think of our Activist CEOs, it's key to consider the support and help around them to inform and channel their path.

Elly continued:

I think my final call is this bit about how to stand up and be counted when you hit a critical boundary, to find those. Making a statement saying I don't agree with this is one thing. Posting hate speech against something is another thing and being willing very clearly to have zero tolerance. Certain kinds of statements, even though we're trying to be tolerant, are really, really important and making things a disciplinary matter early on. A notion of tolerance is everything and therefore we want to be tolerant of everyone's beliefs. That doesn't mean we have to be tolerant of everyone's behaviour.

This is something Reverend Mark, CEO of Tanenbaum, is well versed in:

Many years ago, we created what we now call the Competencies for Respectful Communication about religious diversity. We train people to address behaviour and not belief. So in those moments, when people's beliefs may clash, even about an action that the company is taking, what we can do, what companies can do is manage the behaviours of employees or managers via the standard operating procedures and policies of the company, versus trying to engage people in questions about what they believe because everyone is entitled to believe exactly what they want to.

However, the degree to which there are clear policies and guidance and training for managers and senior executives around how to negotiate those conversations is critically important.

One of the other of our competencies has to do with acknowledging mistakes – apologising and acknowledging mistakes, because here's the thing. I do this work every day, we are all committed to this work. And I would say that we could all admit that at some point during the course of the week, we step in it, we say the wrong thing. We do the wrong thing. We don't think something all the way through or we thought we knew what we were talking about and then got some more information and realise, "Oh, there's more I need to learn about that." Can we create a culture within a company that allows for the apology, allows for that generosity of shared space? If it's not present, then the apology falls flat. So we have to create an environment that allows for employees and managers and senior executives even to be able to take a best faith effort, a good faith effort, if you will, and have it all go wrong, and it not be the end of the conversation.

6

Breathe in Courage, Breathe Out Fear

One of the true joys of doing the work that I do, and leading DIAL Global, isn't just the outward-facing work, where I work with CEOs, diversity leaders, and people leaders to make their organisations a better place for people to thrive, but often the inner work *I* get to do on *myself* when I'm personally inspired by incredible leaders.

One of the women who have taught me so much is Tami Erwin, former Executive Vice President and Group CEO for Verizon Business, now Board Director NYSE, Xerox, John Deere, F5, York and Skylo. She's had a phenomenal career, spanning multiple years of experience in Global Fortune 500 companies, and is a passionate advocate for diversity, inclusion, belonging, and equity and has recently championed multiple initiatives across the board including Verizon's Women's CoLabs, through to a focus on women during the pandemic through to really diving deep into some of the challenges and opportunities within STEM for diverse communities.

And impressive though that sounds, I've barely scratched the surface. Luckily, I've been honoured to spend a lot of time in her company and wanted to bring her story to you.

Tami's Story

"I grew up in a small agricultural community north of Seattle. My father was a physician, but I really thought he was a farmer. So we did a little bit of farming and we did a lot of caregiving in the community in which we lived. I think it was there that I really was grounded to the importance of compassion and kindness and belief that we all are part of a community and therefore we all are part of how we care for one another.

"I started my career at what is now Verizon, some 30 years ago as a customer service rep. I thought I would do that job for a couple of years, and then when I grew up, I would decide what I wanted to do. I don't know that I've fully grown up, but I will tell you that I love the ability to be part of the Verizon mission and our purpose.

"I've had the opportunity to grow through Customer Service, take on large P&L roles, do every field role you could do in Wireless. I spent time in our business really understanding legal and regulatory and some of the labour challenges there. And then I had the opportunity to be our Chief Marketing Officer for a couple of years, so really leaning into "how do you use the brand to differentiate who you are, based on the customers you serve?"

"Then came the ability to come back in now as a CEO of a global business. I have employees in 60 countries around the world. We serve customers in 180 countries around the world. And the thing that's constant for me, as I learned early on in my career, nothing is more important than how we serve customers. But the way you serve customers is through engaged, empowered, excited employees who understand the purpose and a mission.

"As we think about our responsibility then to give back to society and to deliver for our shareholders, it creates a pretty simple framework that has defined from my very beginning the importance of showing up for one another, be it a customer or employee, and then delivering on the commitments that you make to others."

I'm endlessly impressed by her drive and passion, and told her, "You make it sound so simple. I know this is a huge amount of hard work, energy, passion, drive that really goes into making what is a truly successful organisation. And when I say success, I also mean success in the sense of really being compassionate about every person within the organisation and that is our different communities, our ethnically diverse communities. I think this is really a time where we're seeing the very best organisations step up to the mark, the time when we will see organisations that truly care and be remembered for that, with how their leaders behave. I know you're championing a number of different initiatives, tell us about those and how they're implemented."

Tami appears excited to answer this question in particular. "It's interesting, as I think about my career, that we've gone from what has been a pretty polite conversation around diversity, and the need for representation to a much more passionate and urgent conversation about authenticity and creating an environment where people believe they belong.

"It's no longer enough to have representation of gender, representation of age, representation of ethnic backgrounds. It is about creating an environment where each one of us believes we can bring our whole selves into the work environment, and not just be accepted but be embraced for who we are.

"My grandmother was a survivor of domestic violence and Verizon took a very strong position on this, asking how we educate and really help people understand domestic violence so that we can drive prevention and awareness and really create a healthy family environment. And we started that probably 25 years ago, and that was kind of my first foray into taking a strong, committed, passionate position because it was something that I knew personally, my grandmother's experience.

"We went on then to really think about how we think about making sure that we create a work environment that represents the communities in which we live, work, and play.

There are so many elements of that, that you can really get excited about. For me, it's about how we make sure women have an opportunity to have the same kind of leadership roles that our male colleagues play. It's about the ability to compete for those jobs. It's about the ability to be successful at those jobs. And it's the ability to not have to work twice as hard as our male colleagues.

"I'm a huge believer, let me just say it right up front, that men must be part of this conversation. I'm not a man hater. I love them. I want them to be part of the conversation. I want to embrace them as part of the solution. Because if women are only talking to women, we fail to invite the broader population to say, 'this is not a women's issue, this is a leadership and an economic issue'. And only when you unlock the full value of 100% of your team, are you really able to move forward.

"It's the reason why programmes like CoLab become so important. The ability for us to show and share the programmes that we're doing at Verizon that gives women and families the opportunity for flexibility about caregiver leave and the ability to try to balance all the things that life throws in our direction.

"When you think about 2020, and we've taken a tremendous step backwards for women from a career standpoint because women carry an oversized burden of the domestic responsibilities at home. So you think about educating kids, you think about elderly and parent care, you think about what you're trying to do to get meals on the table and keep the house clean and keep the social calendar running. And I for one wouldn't give up those things because it's part of what I love to do as a mom, as a daughter, as a sister, as an aunt, of all the roles that we play.

"Yet we've got to find a way to create more balance for women, more balance for families so that women can show up not just in retail jobs or hospitality jobs or health care, but really have an opportunity to participate actively in STEM and work that's really emerging around science, tech, engineering, math. I see it in my world with 5G as we begin to roll out new technology that will transform the way we live, work, and play. We need men and women actively engaged in building out those applications and solutions. Because only when we do it together, do we really bring forth the best capability.

"We know that corporations that employ women, that boards that have women on them, deliver better performance results. So again, it is not a women's issue. It is a leadership issue. It's an economic issue. We must invite men to be part of that conversation and tap into and unlock the full potential of the team.

"Since the pandemic, there has also been a lot of attention on race. I think about the tragic murder of George Floyd. I think about Asian hate crimes that we saw really accelerate. We have taken a No Tolerance position at Verizon to say, we cannot tolerate violence against anyone. And we have to accelerate our understanding of the cultural differences that we bring into the work environment.

"We've taken a very strong position about taking the time to listen to your colleagues, to get to know what makes them different and unique. Get to understand the holidays, celebrate the foods they eat, the things that make them tremendous parts of our community and celebrate that. If we listen, we can learn, and we can lead with the action. And that action is creating an environment of equality and belonging for everybody."

I wanted to drill down on the issue of allyship, replying, "You talk a lot about the fact that this is obviously not just a female issue, but a male issue. It's that allyship that you describe that makes it so terribly important. Yes, technically speaking, we have around about 50% of the population that are female, and then we have those that would not be male or female. However, how much change can we make, as simple as it sounds, by preaching to the converted? We must welcome, as you said, every individual, no matter what race, no matter what background, the visible diversities, the invisible diversities. We must take this absolute stand that says, 'No more. Absolutely no more.' I wonder whether you could share some of the kind of the real pivotal moments that you have seen and experienced, particularly when working out there with your communities?"

"First of all," Tami firmly replies, "One of the things that I love most about my job is the ability to be in front of my customers, be in front of my employees. Then I really feel in touch with the business, that I can listen to what my employees are experiencing. I can watch them in action with customers. I can listen to customers and better understand their requirements. We can really, truly partner to move the business forward and, at the end of the day, I have a leadership philosophy – a couple of critical leadership philosophies – that I believe to be true.

"You don't serve the customer directly, you are in service of those that do and that's likely due to my customer service routes. The fact that I started in the role of serving customers means I have tremendous respect and appreciation for the jobs that we ask our frontline employees to do because they are the employees that bring our brand to life, are the ones that take the things that we build and translate that to customers and really create the personalised customer experience.

"I have, my entire career, spent a tremendous amount of time in the field because I have great respect and appreciation for what people do. I also have a belief that my job is to serve those who serve, that I work for my frontline employees. My job is to make sure they have the tools and the resources and the information, as opposed to being the Inspector General. Yes, I'm always looking for what we can do better but my job is to create an environment where the teams have clarity of purpose, of the mission. We've defined our purposes, creating the networks that move the world forward. And if that's our purpose, does every employee understand where they fit and how they belong?

"One of the most pivotal moments for me, as we think about women in leadership roles, occurred years ago. I was hosting what we call our President's Cabinet trip. It was a beautiful evening in Rome and we were celebrating our top sales performers. And it was the time I was the COO for our Wireless business. As I stood at the front of the room and I watched our top sales performers come forward, what I realised is 85% of our top sales performers were men. And it struck me that night something was wrong. And as I went back into the work environment after that celebration, I started to dig into the data. And what I found is that women hesitate to sign up for a job where it's a quota-based job and they're putting compensation at risk, because they often have lacked the confidence to believe that their performance will enable them to not only deliver what they can but really excel in a sales position. And as I dug deeper into the data, what I found was that 85% of our sales associates were men, 90% of our sales managers were men. So I had to ask, how can we create an environment for women to be successful at sales? How do we create this and avoid having hunters and gatherers?

"We went back and created a programme and called it Women of Wireless. It was a programme that allowed us to help women really build their competence capabilities, build their personal brand, declare what their intent was for their career, learn to network, improve their communication skills, all things that women needed to really practise. And then we moved women into sales positions as they raised their hand and said, 'I want to do this.' We've seen incredibly strong performance of women that are declaring their intent, moving into sales and moving in with competence, then into management roles, because from our sales teams, we create managers from our managers, we've great senior leaders, and so it has been a tremendous programme.

"When we reset our organisation two years ago, we moved the programme from Women of Wireless to Women of the World. It's now a global programme that is for women in sales and non-sales roles who want to make a year-long investment. They apply for it. They're sponsored. They have SWAT teams. It's become an incredibly, incredibly powerful programme, all because one night I watched and observed and said, 'Something is wrong, and something must change.'

"It's one of those programmes where I look at that and go, 'I'm really proud because it will have a lasting impact on how we think about the acceleration of women in sales roles and women in senior roles.'

"One of the things that I have found in my work is that when you take the forward motion of planting a seed, people will immediately gravitate around you and say, 'Yes, there is a need', and they'll jump in and be part of building a programme. They'll accelerate the sponsorship of people that are in the programme. They'll make it bigger and better than you thought it needed to be and that's the power of bringing together a group of women and men in our programme.

"We asked men to be part of the programme to understand their role as sponsors, to understand their role as leaders, to really have the conversations with all employees, men, women, particularly diversity candidates to say 'What is it you want to do with your career? How can I help you build that development plan, take some ownership and accountability?' It's always amazing to me – you plant the seed, you create the environment and people run with a mission, when you tap into the right mission."

Tami's words made me think of the phrase, "from little acorns do big oak trees grow", and I said to her, "You mentioned there, diverse candidates and those that come from different backgrounds. I think it is so incredibly valuable to recognise, as not only do women have additional responsibilities but you then look at the socio-demographics that people come from, the locations that people come from, it's very much this difference between quality versus equality and that recognition that some people need to have an additional step up – and it is putting in programmes such as the ones that you described to allow everyone to flourish and allow them to succeed, to actually help and support us all to get to that place of success and wider community."

Tami agreed, adding, "I think that's so well said, because everybody has a different experience in their life. They've had different influences, moments, different times in their life and defined who they are. There's a lot written right now about unconscious biases. I think we have to be much more aware of the unconscious biases that become part of who we are. So we can be open and listen and learn.

"What we know about the difference between men and women is that men tend to be, by nature, more confident. If you ask a man and a woman to look at a list of 10 things that qualify them for a job, a male will look at the list and say, 'I think I've got seven of those. I'm wildly qualified', and a woman is likely to look at that same list and go, 'I've got nine and a half, I'm not sure I'm fully qualified.'

"We know that men historically have been promoted based on potential and women have been promoted based on proving that they're capable. And that's just a harsh reality in our environment. And if we as women can learn to say, 'I am qualified, I am enough, I'm great at what I do', and recognise the skills and capabilities, we then not only become the most qualified candidates, we can deliver results with confidence. And we don't feel like we're always playing catch-up.

"That's my goal for women – is that they feel like they can not only be a mom and a daughter and a sister and aunts and all the roles we play, but we can do that and feel great about the careers that we have."

I was completely on board with everything Tami was saying, and then she said something so profound that she provided me with another reason for me to carry on the work I do. Because despite all the things that make us different, our shared humanity has never been more important.

"If we think forward to the future, and we think about what's happening with the fourth industrial revolution and really where tech is changing our world, we want men and women, we want diversity of age and gender and race and experience to be creating the world of the future as we think about how tech will change everything.

"We are dealing with so many big societal issues, whether it's environment, whether it's the unrest that we see around the world, whether it's a digital divide from an education standpoint, we've got to make sure that we've got the entirety of the world working against the world's biggest problems and we're certainly committed to doing that at Verizon and we realise it takes all of us playing together to be able to accomplish that.

"There are three or four things I think are so important for every one of us as we think about what we want to do with our career. And, first of all, I believe many of us can accomplish whatever we choose to do. So be your biggest cheerleader and recognise if you want something, absolutely you can achieve it. But there's some things that you're going to have to do along the way.

"Number one is, face fear head on. The reality is every one of us has things that we fear, and I've had to ask myself, what's the worst thing that could happen? And once you ask yourself that, you can face your fear pretty directly and pretty head on. I have a saying that I share with my team, which is a basic principle of breathing, and being intentional about taking a deep breath. I say, breathe in courage and breathe out fear.

"The second one, I think it's particularly important for women but it's important for everyone, and that is practise good self-care. If we fail to put on our own oxygen mask first, how do we make sure that we steal from our emotional bank account so that we have plenty to give? Because it's only when you feel filled that you feel like you can give. One of the things that I've worked hard on over the years with my own family is practising bringing home the best of me at the end of the day, rather than the leftovers. Don't package up the leftovers and bring what's left over home. Bring the best of you, and the way you do that is by practising good self-care.

"And the third one is invite men to be part of this conversation. Do not exclude men from the conversation, so that we're all talking about and putting a spotlight on not just women in the workforce, but diversity, inclusion, authenticity. It's time to drop the masks that we all wear and bring a true version of who we are to the work environment and embrace that because we'll find it when we bring the best of who we are to work – people aren't faking it. They can be real, they can be authentic, and they can feel as though they belong and when people feel that they belong and that they're valued, they'll do anything to help accomplish the mission. So face fear head on, practise self-care, bring men into the conversation because only when we fully unlock diversity, inclusion, authenticity, that we can demonstrate equality and belonging for everybody."

7

Go Blaze a Trail of Your Own

Leadership is hard to define and good leadership even harder. But if you can get people to follow you to the ends of the earth, you are a great leader.

They're the words of Indra Nooyi, the first woman of colour to run a Fortune 50 company. She was CEO of PepsiCo for 12 years and during that time the company increased its profitability and improved its environmental sustainability.

Mary Barra was the first woman to lead General Motors. She told the world, "If we win the hearts and minds of employees, we're going to have better business success."

Safra Catz is the CEO of global software company Oracle, and maybe has a more sanguine perspective on being a woman in business. "The most significant barrier to female leadership is the actual lack of females in leadership. The best advice I can give to women is to go out and start something, ideally their own businesses. If you can't see a path for leadership within your company, go blaze a trail of your own."

All powerful quotes from powerful, impressive women. But, in 2024, where do we stand when it comes to gender equality? While the dial hasn't moved anywhere near as far as it should quite yet, there has been a certain degree of movement within the sphere.

We *are* seeing more senior females in leadership, and we are seeing it more widely talked about, but if we look at the demographics within the FTSE and in the Fortune organisations, they are still mainly run by middle-aged White guys, and the rare females who *are* in positions of power are White.

November 2022 saw new research launched by Cranfield School of Management. Women account for almost 40% of directors on FTSE 100 boards and 39% on FTSE 250 boards, but they found an "appalling" lack of progress of women into executive roles.

For the third year in a row, only 47 women hold executive directorships in the FTSE 250, while it has increased by just 3% to 36 in the FTSE 100 in the last year.

Some 91% of women on FTSE 100 boards are in Non-Executive Director roles but just nine women hold CEO roles in the FTSE 100. While the number of women on FTSE 100 boards continued to rise, the lack of progress of women into key executive roles suggests the increase was thanks to boards appointing female Non-Executive Directors (NEDs) to comply with targets.

The Female FTSE Board Report 2022 revealed that ten companies in the FTSE 100 have 30% or less female representation. Of the 413 directorships held by women across the FTSE 100, just nine were CEOs, 18 were Chairs, and 377 were NEDs. The number of women in NED roles in the FTSE 100 has increased by 15% over the past year, whereas women in executive directorships increased by just 3% to 36.

Meanwhile in the FTSE 250, the number of women on boards has increased from 35% to 39% year-on-year, with 110 companies already meeting the 40% target. But for the third year running, only 47 women hold executive directorships in the FTSE 250.

Alison Kay, Managing Partner for Client Service at EY, UK & Ireland, said:

> *The research shows that FTSE businesses are increasingly hitting the targets set for female representation. However, they are falling woefully short of the intended outcome – distributing the power and influence necessary to achieve true gender parity. My observation is that companies have exhausted all the so-called "low-hanging fruit" and now it is time for tough decisions to push further into root and branch reform.*
>
> *The gender pay gap has long been, rightly, a huge marker of inequality which I still can't believe I'm writing about in 2023. Recent*

figures around the closing of the gap have been slightly less easy to inter-pret due to the impact of the pandemic, furlough and the fact that the majority of childcare and caring responsibilities feel to women, who were disproportionately affected by the crisis.

The ONS has released gender pay gap figures for 2023, and stated the gap "has been declining slowly over time. Over the last decade it has fallen by approximately a quarter among both full-time employees and all employees."

In 2023, the gap among full-time employees increased to 7.7%, up from 7.6% in 2022. This is still below the gap of 9.0% before the coronavirus (COVID-19) pandemic in 2019. Among all employees, the gender pay gap decreased to 14.3% in 2023, from 14.4% in 2022, and is still below the levels seen in 2019 (17.4%).

It still shocks me that it was only in 2017 that mandatory gender pay gap (GPG) reporting was introduced. Response to it has been mixed, mainly around the fact it overlooks complexities such as part-time work and family structures.

The Trades Union Congress (TUC) came out with some startling research in February 2024[1] – that the average woman effectively works for free for nearly two months of the year.

The gender pay gap for all employees is 15.4%, meaning, according to the TUC, women wait 56 days before they start to get paid on Women's Pay Day. In *education*, the gender pay gap is 25.4%, so the average woman effectively works for free for more than a quarter of the year and in *health care and social work* jobs, where the gender pay gap is 18.3%, the average woman waits 67 days for her Women's Pay Day.

The United Nations published a report on the impact of gender inequality globally[2] – again in the shadow of the COVID-19 pandemic. They stated:

A new global analysis of progress on gender equality and women's rights shows women and girls remain disproportionately affected by the socio-economic fallout from the COVID-19 pandemic, struggling with disproportionately high job and livelihood losses, education disruptions and increased burdens of unpaid care work. Women's health services, poorly funded even before the pandemic, faced major disruptions, undermining women's sexual and reproductive health. And despite women's central role in responding to COVID-19, including as front-line health workers, they are still largely bypassed for leadership positions they deserve.

This is, of course, in addition to the other inequalities facing women and girls before the pandemic hit.

As of 2023, an estimated 338 million women and girls around the world are living in extreme poverty, with women's food insecurity levels 10% higher than men's in 2020, compared with 6% higher in 2019.

In early 2022, the World Bank released its *Women, Business and the Law* report.[3] It stated around 2.4 billion women of working age "are not afforded equal economic opportunity and 178 countries maintain legal barriers that prevent their full economic participation".

Its data stated that "in 86 countries, women face some form of job restriction and 95 countries do not guarantee equal pay for equal work", and globally, women still have only three-quarters of the legal rights afforded to men".

And before women even get to the workplace, they're on the back foot. According to UNICEF, 129 million girls are out of school globally, and in countries affected by conflict, girls are more than twice as likely to be out of school than girls living in non-affected countries.[4] In many countries, girls are seen as second-class citizens, so education is a luxury not afforded to them, and indeed many human rights are denied purely because of their gender, for example, enforced child marriage.

The statistics I've just laid bare in front of you are a tiny overview of a handful of reports available on global and domestic inequality. The tip of the iceberg of a huge, societal and endlessly debated crisis which can be demonstrated to the uneducated through colourful graphs and pie charts, numbers leaping out from a nicely designed PowerPoint presentation.

DIAL Global's Diversity Review found that 2023, in the UK, one in three (34%, up from 23%) of participating UK companies say they have at least 50% female representation on their senior leadership team. Companies continue to focus on this, with four in five participating UK companies saying they specify gender diversity in leadership succession planning (82%) and almost nine in ten track progress towards it (89%, up from 75%).

Gender ranks 6th of all 10 facets. Although most participating UK companies have focused on gender diversity for years, progress remains slow. Jo Portlock, VP Diversity & Inclusion at Lexis Nexis Risk Solutions, told us:

> *Gender equity is fundamental to any inclusive culture. As a technology and data company, we don't have the easiest start point to our gender balance. We need to continue to understand and manage gender parity to ensure we remain competitive and innovative. For us, gender equity involves understanding and removing barriers, we have high flexible working practices, sponsorship, and mentor connections, 10 gender-based employee resource groups, menopause support networks and parenting mentorship. In recent years we have increased our representation of women in top leadership, line management, sales, and technology, whilst improving our retention of women at all levels.*

Joanna Allen, CEO of Graze, told us, "Progress is being made but female CEOs remain the minority. Our focus to realise gender diversity on leadership teams must include female representation in roles with financial responsibility and strategic impact within their remit, rather than being satisfied simply with leadership team representation."

It's a slightly different picture in the US. Gender parity at the senior level is increasing, although still only one in three (30%) of participating US companies say they have at least 50% female representation on their senior leadership team. Companies continue to focus on this, with four in five participating US companies saying they specify gender diversity in leadership succession planning (88%) and almost five in six tracking progress towards it (83%).

Gender ranks 3rd in all facets. Although most participating US companies have focused on gender diversity for years, progress appears to have stalled. Dr Yetta Toliver is the Global Head of Diversity, Inclusion and Belonging at XEROX Corporation and told DIAL:

> *It is good news that gender parity did improve. Within our organization, we are focusing on achieving parity through the hiring, developing, promoting and retaining women for leadership positions. Yet, research indicates phenomena such as the "broken rung" and "glass cliff" make it challenging for women to advance into senior leadership positions. It is important to remove these types of barriers from within the organization.*

It's also been alarming to see the number of high-profile women quitting top jobs.

YouTube CEO Susan Wojcicki, one of Google's earliest employees, announced she was leaving to "start a new chapter focused on my family, health, and personal projects I'm passionate about".

Meta confirmed CBO Marne Levine was bidding farewell to "recharge and prioritize some quality time with family", making her the third female C-suite leader to leave

Meta in recent years, following the departure of Sheryl Sandberg and Carolyn Everson.

Alexis Krivkovich is an author of the McKinsey Lean In "Women in the Workplace" report,[5] and told CNN "for every woman stepping into a director-level leadership role, two are choosing to leave".

She continued:

The pattern has the potential to unwind decades of progress toward gender equity and increased female leadership in the workplace. It's a huge concern and worth focusing on.

They are doing more in their roles than men are typically doing across a whole gamut of things that support their office culture and community. They do twice as much sponsorship support, spend more time on diversity work, and spend more time mentoring and sponsoring colleagues within the organization.

Lots of men leave their positions, but we analyse and scrutinize when women leaders do in a different way. If we had a lot more women prime ministers and CEOs and leaders at the very top, when we had one retire or exit, it wouldn't feel like such a loss.

But, of course, there are also good news stories out there. There's something in the water at Severn Trent and United Utilities – both of which have female CEOs. Indeed, in 2023, Severn Trent was recognised in the Bloomberg Gender-Equality Index (GEI) for the fourth year running. The GEI recognises a company's commitment to solving gender inequality through policy development, and much like DIAL's 10 Facets, or our S Framework, searches for equality across five pillars: (1) leadership and talent pipeline; (2) equal pay and gender pay parity; (3) inclusive culture policies; (4) anti-sexual harassment policies; and (5) external brand. Severn Trent received its highest ever score at 74%.

In response to the GEI news, Liv Garfield, CEO of Severn Water, said:

> *We firmly believe that a diverse business is a more successful one, so it's important that we create a workforce that's fair for everyone. It means we can provide a better service for customers, as diversity helps us truly understand the communities we serve and operate in.*
>
> *This global recognition is another proud moment for us, and shows we're clearly heading in the right direction and doing the right things when it comes to addressing gender inequality.*
>
> *It will always be a key focus for us to address equality and create a fair and equal workplace, and we'll continue to play our part in building a fairer society.*

In a piece Garfield wrote for FTSE Women Leaders,[6] it was the culture of the organisation which she is particularly proud of:

> *The same is true in our approach to diversity, we are only ever as good as the last action we agreed, the last decision that we took or the choice that we made. It matters how we hold ourselves to account on every appointment, on every promotion, on pay, on training and opportunity. But it also matters how we show up at work each day, how we think about the world, the way in which we make decisions and the way we organise ourselves. Because, for me, that is the essence of both diversity and inclusion.*
>
> *When it comes to our gender diversity, we've much to be proud of, but there is always more to be done. I work with brilliant women role models on the board, the Executive and across the leadership and management teams, yet despite significant steps forward, we are still underrepresented in some operational roles and we need to inspire young women to see the amazing opportunities that exist. And, of course, to continue our work to increase the representation of black, Asian and other ethnically diverse women, particularly in senior management and leadership roles, where across businesses they remain even more underrepresented than white women.*

Louise Beardmore runs United Utilities, a CEO keen to put the S into ESG. She told Leadership Consultants Hoggett Bowers,[7] it's a key priority:

We're proud to be signatories to the UN Race to Zero campaign. We are actively contributing to the UK water industry's commitment to be net zero from 2030. As part of our route to net zero, in 2020, we made six carbon pledges including our tree pledge, renewables, green fleet pledge, peat pledge, emissions pledge and partnership pledge – we're working together with our suppliers and employees to prevent the worst impacts of climate change.

The great thing about my job is that I focus on the needs of employees and customers and often those needs are the same. The North West was hit really hard with COVID and our employees also felt those challenges.

We launched our Staff Outreach Scheme (UU SOS), a fund which an employee could apply for to receive a one-off payment of up to £5,000 to help ease some of the significant financial burden they and their family experienced because of the effect of COVID.

Senior Directors also sacrificed some of their salary to enable over 150,000 meals to be provided to the food bank to help customers in the North West who were struggling financially too but it's not just about financial support.

In partnership with the MIND charity, we have also launched two e-learning packages to complement the existing training, support, and resources. These courses help our employees to identify signs of poor mental health in themselves and others, and provide them with the additional support and resource they may need to support good mental health.

Our mental health support and provision have increased significantly over the last couple of months, and this is something we are committed to continuing.

I've also been finding it fascinating to see that the women who are breaking the glass ceiling are also doing so in unexpected sectors. The hiring of Jennie Daly as the first female CEO of a FTSE 100 housebuilder (Taylor Wimpey) shows that an industry seen as male-dominated is also becoming more gender-inclusive.

According to a recent piece in *Forbes*, women remain underrepresented in finance and accountancy, despite entering in equal numbers to men. Margherita Della Valle is the CEO at Vodafone Group, hired in 2023 after being promoted from CFO.

She was so determined to see women in finance roles, she launched an initiative called NXT GEN Women in Finance, with sponsors who now identify, mentor, and promote female rising stars in finance.

"I think there are the same types of obstacles and challenges in finance, as in other functions within an organisation," she told *Forbes*.

"A fundamental obstacle is what people call 'subconscious bias'. The definition of leadership, and the leadership attributes that people are looking for, are still very much male-dominated in nature. This colours daily interactions and promotions and also women's own engagement when pushing their careers. Sometimes you see women just disconnecting from the game, because it's not the game they want to play."[8]

Echoing Safra Catz, Valle says:

The solution to this problem is going to be more women in leadership roles and diversity at every level. That's the real game-changer we all need to push for. For example, a couple of years ago I witnessed a training session on how women should behave in interviews if they want to be successful. In my opinion, it's not the women who need to change to be successful in interviews. It's the interviewers who need to change and the nature of the interviews needs to be different. A lot of the advice that women get in terms of selling their competencies and looking confident might be different if the interviewers themselves were women. I believe personally that I interview differently from men.

Debra Crew is the CEO of drinks giant Diageo. She, alongside Louise Prashad, the Chief HR Officer, Rachel Toner, the Strategy and Transformation Project, and Karen Blackett OBE, a Non-Executive Director, have been recognised in Involve's Heroes Role Model Lists 2023.

Diageo's Society 2030: Spirit of Progress' goals plan to achieve 50% representation of women in leadership roles by 2030. Since Louise's appointment, Diageo has introduced new guidelines and policies aimed at creating the most supportive and inclusive environment possible. They also have the UK Spirited Women Network, Diageo's Employee Resource Group which hosts engagements, such as an event with the charity Tommy's to discuss how we can support colleagues through pregnancy loss.

As of June 2023, 73% of the board is female, and Diageo has implemented schemes to help promote gender equality. Pregnancy Loss Guidelines, Fertility Support Guidelines, and "Thriving through Menopause" are all initiatives created to support women.

The pharma sector has also hired its first female CEO. GlaxoSmithKline is now being headed up by Emma Walmsley, and in an interview with her I read recently, she epitomises an Activist CEO:

We should be much more proactive about sponsoring and supporting all types of diversity to get to the senior leadership positions.

You cannot be a modern employer in an industry that should be future-facing and modernising (arguably much more aggressively than it is) without being very demanding on this topic.

In practice, this means understanding and responding to the needs of patients and healthcare workers in all our markets. And attracting and supporting a workforce that reflects the diverse communities we both operate in and collaborate with. We're highly committed to flexible working. Our staff face changing requirements and demands at different stages of their lives and, where possible, we'll respond with flexible solutions. We're also looking at attitudes that may create barriers to gender equity in our senior roles, and empowering individuals to enact change.

Milena Mondini de Focatiis is Group Chief Executive Officer of Admiral. In their recent Ethnicity Pay Gap Report,[9] she restated her commitment to inclusivity and belonging:

One of the pillars our business was founded on 30 years ago was equality, and we work hard to foster an inclusive workplace where everyone feels they can thrive and reach their full potential. I believe this is key to creating a more diverse workplace.

I'm really proud that 94% of our colleagues believe that Admiral is a diverse and inclusive employer. For us, being a great place to work means prioritising an honest and transparent culture and I'm pleased that, for the first time, we can publish our ethnicity pay gap data. Over 80% of our colleagues have chosen to share their ethnicity data with us. Our figures reflect the fact that we have a higher proportion of colleagues from ethnically diverse backgrounds working in functions which attract higher salaries, such as IT, Data, Finance and Technology. We're committed to ensuring that all of our teams represent the customers and communities which we serve.

In an interview with *Business Live*, Milena stressed the need to get more women into senior roles in organisations.[10]

The data shows that there is a problem, and although we are making a lot of progress, there is still a legacy of that culture and, in different countries, to a varying extent. There are a lot of things companies can do to solve this. To me, a lot is about recruiting and identifying talent. It is about getting under the skin of people beyond the level of confidence they project, as this is an area sometimes where women don't project as much as men in the recruiting space, and then supporting them through all stages within the company. It is also, of course, about leading by example.

Rosalind Brewer, former CEO of Walgreens Boots Alliance, was at one point one of only two Black female CEOs of Fortune 500 companies (and when she left, Thasunda Brown Duckett became the *only* Black female CEO of a Fortune 500) and says bringing her whole self to work has been the key to her success. She told *Harvard Business Review*, she is "adamant about making sure that I am clear about my role, what my intent is, and how do I bring together my toolbox".[11]

I think the one thread that I can pull through all of my roles and opportunities is my personal leadership, and that's the way I show up first and foremost. Because most of these business problems that I face in these leadership roles, it takes character, it takes guts, it takes problem solving, and when I bring that basic toolkit to bear in these different roles, it has been proven effective for me every time.

Sometimes it's a lonely position because you don't see yourself in different environments that you're in, and then I look at myself personally and say, what can I do to change this because it could be difficult at certain times? I think that the environment is opening up more to people recognizing the differences and appreciating the differences.

One of the things that I think about when I'm thinking about diversity is diversity of thought. Because we can also realize that there are individuals who may not be of diverse culture, race, or gender themselves, but where is their mindset? How do they think about different cultures and different environments?

One of the things that I began to do in my career is to put agile teams together. And what I mean by that is, a lot of times, you have your finance team working in their silo. You'll have the tech team working in their silo. But what I really think works is when we create these agile teams and put them against the biggest problems to solve.

And so, when you put that team together, you are forcing finance and technology and operations and manufacturing all to be in the same room, in the same discussion, against the biggest problem to solve. And it's not finance solving a finance problem. What that actually does: it gets the diversity of thought to happen. And then you have different people sitting around the table. And in some cases, one of the outcomes that I've seen is that in certain functions, we have heavier opportunity for diversity than we do in others.

Many times I am called upon and asked to give my opinion on diversity issues, I am as frank as I possibly can be, because I do think I hold a unique position. When I get in these settings I take advantage of an opportunity to learn and educate those around me, because I can feel it when they're unfamiliar with me or my culture. I don't hide my culture. I talk about it very openly. I feel like that is almost my second reason for being. Everybody has their purpose in how you get into a situation or an environment, but I take advantage of it and do everything I can to teach and expose people to my culture and who I am.

Karen Lynch is the president and CEO of CVS and I've loved watching her career flourish. She's been ranked first on Fortune's Most Powerful Women List for the past two years, and unsurprisingly so, considering she heads up a pharma retail giant, CVS Health, which administered the COVID-19 vaccine in more than 40,000 care facilities and supported the most vulnerable communities in the US by teaming up with partners such as Lyft to provide the vaccine to those most in need. She's also reduced the prices of sanitary products to help stamp out period inequality. I saw a quote from her which has resonated with me, and which I now remind myself of regularly:

"Be authentic. Be yourself, and work at places that really welcome who you are. You'll get up every single morning passionately committed to making a difference. Leave your fingerprints. Really think about . . . what's the impact that I had because of this job?"

And considering we started looking at the facet with the words of Indra Nooyi, I'd like to wrap up with another incredible quote from her too:

"Just because you are CEO, don't think you have landed. You must continually increase your learning, the way you think, and the way you approach the organization. I've never forgotten that."

Notes

1. https://www.tuc.org.uk/news/tuc-gender-pay-gap-means-women-work-first-two-months-year-unpaid
2. https://www.unwomen.org/en/news/stories/2021/10/feature-what-does-gender-equality-look-like-today
3. https://wbl.worldbank.org/content/dam/sites/wbl/documents/2021/02/WBL2022%20Chapter%201.pdf
4. https://www.unicef.org/education/girls-education#:~:text=In%20countries%20affected%20by%20conflict,gender%20parity%20in%20primary%20education.
5. https://leanin.org/women-in-the-workplace/2022#!
6. ftsewomenleaders.com/inspiring-women/liv-garfield
7. www.hoggett-bowers.com/the-hoggett-bowers-2...
8. https://www.forbes.com/sites/sallypercy/2022/03/22/vodafone-finance-chief-margherita-della-valle-i-want-to-see-more-female-cfos/
9. admiralgroup.co.uk/ethnicity-pay-gap-report-2023
10. www.business-live.co.uk/enterprise/naples...
11. https://hbr.org/2021/12/walgreens-ceo-roz-brewer-to-leaders-put-your-phones-away-and-listen-to-employees#:~:text=But%20I%20will%20tell%20you,I%20bring%20together%20my%20toolbox.

8

The Three Steves

In my interview with Tami Erwin, she was adamant that one of her three key lessons in leadership was ensuring men are invited into diversity and inclusion conversations. Which takes me nicely to three men who are three brilliant leaders. Three allies who believe in change, inclusion, and leading from the front. The men who spearheaded DIAL Global's Activist Council.

The Three Steves. Steve Murrells, then CEO of the Co-op, Steve Rowe from M&S, and Steve Ingham from Page Group. I've had the incredible opportunity to work alongside these men through running DIAL Global, working with them on our initiatives, and interviewing them for our summits and launch events.

All white, middle-class and male the fact they even shared the same name always caused to giggle whenever they appeared together to talk about any aspect of diversity and inclusion!

However, they shared far more important things than just these attributes.

They all recognise that change was happening too slowly.

It must be led from the top and become pervasive throughout their organisations.

They would make personal mistakes on the way, but this could not be an excuse to do nothing and was in fact an important part of learning.

They willing to share this learning freely to help others and create platforms to advance the agenda across-the-board.

They recognised there was no silver bullet and leaders had to take a long-term and holistic view to make a difference.

That more diverse inclusive organisations were imperative to building a good business of any sort.

Steve Rowe was always adamant about his commitment to creating diverse and inclusive workplaces and driving social mobility for the benefit of shareholders, colleagues, customers and the community:

> *Marks and Spencer is truly a diverse business operating across the whole of the UK, and in many parts of the globe, 1000s of different products and services for millions of different customers, located in a wide range of communities. M&S has always been at its most successful when it's relevant to the communities that it lives and works in, it's as simple as that. And the UK is a very diverse place.*
>
> *Diversity gives you different thoughts. And I believe without differences or differences of opinion, you become a weaker business in how you solve for the customer. That's the business imperative but let's be clear, our colleagues are demanding more diversity and more inclusivity, customers demand more inclusivity and more diversity, and so will our investors soon – so we have to make sure we deliver change.*
>
> *Too many businesses were paying lip service to a diverse and inclusive agenda.*

As someone who heads up a recruitment organisation, Steve Ingham couldn't agree more:

> *We're talking to candidates about their reasons why they would leave a business. And I think a lot of leaders forget this. The reality is they're leaving businesses because they don't feel they're diverse enough or doing enough in the community. They don't take on responsibility for social responsibility. They're probably not doing enough for the environment and sustainability, and these are the reasons people are leaving. At the same time the leaders are talking about a shortage of talent and so we've got to get both right.*
>
> *Personally, why I'm passionate about it stemmed from 30 years ago when one of my top-performing individuals asked to have a private meeting with me. He came out to me, and I asked, "Why do you need to tell me?" He said, "Well, I haven't felt comfortable. I'd been agonising with this for several years. I didn't feel people around me would necessarily feel*

comfortable with it." I was shocked and realised how difficult it must be if you've got a difference, if you are relating to a certain facet of diversity and you don't feel comfortable that you can be yourself at work. That is awful.

I've got three daughters and I want to make sure there's a level playing field for them. The thought that they would be paid less or overlooked for an opportunity in favour of a man would make me furious, for obvious reasons. The commercial reality of when we lose women in business, who are trained, who are high performers, who want to do the most natural thing in the world and have children to expand their family but feel they have to leave to do that to be a good mum – that's ridiculous.

Steve has always been very open about his own changing identity.

A couple of years ago I myself became disabled. I realised the inequality that exists there as well, far fewer people who are disabled work. And when they do work, they're paid less and that is absolutely, morally wrong. And at a time where we've got candidate shortages and talent shortages, it's incredible how we forget this pool of talent, which is 14%. How can we ignore that talent pool? So many people with disabilities have got more courage, more resilience, more energy than a lot of people who are able-bodied than that, and I think we really should be looking at making sure we bring those diversities into all facets into our businesses.

Steve Murrells refers to this as "it's all about a head and a heart, isn't it?" and he's quite right. He states, "Diversity is great business sense. The head part is those businesses with a more diverse workforce are better than those that aren't. And the heart part is, probably through all of our personal journeys, that we know this is the right thing to do and to champion and to educate people in the right way and provide the right information and answers for them."

As my background is in recruitment, and one of the reasons I pivoted my expertise was because I was frustrated

with people hiring in their own image, I was really struck by
Steve Rowe talking about talent shortages:

> *I think this talent shortage is really important, and too many businesses
> are fishing in one part of the pond and they're fishing in Russell Group
> and Oxbridge for graduate talent. Frankly, the talent's all over the
> country. It's in every community, in every level of education. I don't have
> a degree, for example, and one of the things I want my business to do is
> to look carefully at where there are groups of talented young individuals.*
>
> *We have to make our businesses accessible to everybody, and it
> really is about accessibility. And we need to make sure that people can see
> the career paths within our organisations, for people like them. One of
> the things I've noticed about Marks and Spencer is there are not enough
> senior roles that are truly diverse. We have lots of diversity through the
> organisation but once you get through the middle management, I am
> not happy that we've got diversity in every one of the key roles.*
>
> *You have to make those careers fast, accessible for everybody, and
> attractive to everybody. Otherwise, frankly, we're going to miss a huge
> pool of talent, we will not be diverse and not represent the communities
> we live in. We have to make sure we've got mobility in every way across
> the organisation.*

Steve Murrells, on the issue of CEOs working together
to amplify change, says it's so important for leaders to come
together, to share ideas, to work on issues together, as CEOs
"set the tone, the drumbeat in all of our organisations". He
continued:

> *In order for this to really be credible and to change things, you want it
> flowing through the entire organisation. There are some important
> lessons that I've learned on this journey since we started to talk about
> this issue at that terrible moment when George Floyd died in
> Minneapolis.*
>
> *You can't rush this. You've got to put yourself in a place of under-
> standing of what it feels like to be on the receiving end of these issues.
> What this boils down to is that talent is everywhere, but opportunity*

isn't. What we're trying to do is to create pathways for everybody to have the same life chances that everyone else has got. But, in order to do that, in these areas of real inclusion, you've got to get underneath the skin. You've got to understand what it means to be a black person or a person of disability or a different sexual orientation. Only then will you be able to make the changes that you need to make in the organisation so that it doesn't become a "tick box".

All three of us could go and employ tens of thousands of individuals tomorrow, and they would fail. And they would fail for the simple reason that culturally and structurally, we've got to learn how to work with a more ethnic, diverse, inclusive workforce.

Here we are – three white men. How could we possibly know what it feels like to be on the receiving end of racism as an example? We couldn't. What we can do is listen, what we can do is then make change and build the community so that when we look back in our businesses in 10 or 15 years' time, and we can see the legacy of a far more diverse workforce.

Along that journey, our role as leaders as part of the DIAL Global Activist CEO pledge is to effectively tell the story, to shine the light on this issue today. It's just the right thing to do.

Steve Ingham picked up on this point, adding, "The key to that success is authenticity, and not just a one-off piece of authenticity, but actually being consistently authentic every single year, in every message you do, in every facet of your vision and your strategy. Then you can really start to make a difference in your business and maybe in others."

One of the reasons I've loved launching one of DIAL's stand-out initiatives, the Activist Council, with the Three Steves, is because of their lived experiences and their passion to bring new ideas to the table. Steve Ingham has long talked about needing the support of government.

"We disclose pay gap differences, why not disability? There is one, and I think companies should have to be open about it. If the government doesn't make that legislation, maybe we should do it anyway and a group of CEOs could potentially challenge others to get on board."

Steve Murrells certainly echoes that point. He says:

Whether we're trailblazers of three or trailblazers of many, we do need some government thinking on this as well to help us punch through.

We issued one of the largest surveys on youth. This generation is sitting there after COVID feeling hopeless and disengaged, and it's going to be up to us, to government, and local leaders to create a better future for them, who, at the moment when you ask them, are completely disillusioned. How we can beat the drum, how we can move towards government as well as every other business is absolutely the right thing to do.

It's not quick. I think we all have to recognise that. This is a bit like climate change. We've got our act, an act now. We're going to have to do it together because it's bigger than one business, but it's going to take our lifetime to get it right.

Steve Rowe added:

I think the true systemic change has to be led from the top. There's no other way to do it. I have had a lot to learn personally, and I have to be clean. I'm a middle-aged white Steve, with privilege in pretty much every respect. Understanding how that's different to every experience that others might have had is a bit scary! None of us wants to make mistakes, none of us wants to be seen as stupid. Being able to show that you're not seeing tackling the issue because you're ignorant – it takes a bit of courage.

What's good about having collaboration is, I can learn from the other Steves, we can share where we've been stronger, where we've made mistakes. But also, can colleagues look up and say, "Is the Governor doing it? Is he willing to put himself on the line? Is he scared about this or not? And is he going to make a difference?" If they can't see that, there is absolutely no way they will join the fray. We cannot give up.

I take a great deal of time to have reverse mentoring. I've got a couple of lovely colleagues who give me safe space to learn. They take me to task on behalf of the business on a regular basis, which is great. And we've moved from what I would say was a fairly pedestrian diversity inclusion programme to taking serious action on every front.

One of the most comforting and supportive messages Steve Murrells had for other CEOs was about the bravery of not always getting it right. "Remember, we will get this wrong. But we shouldn't worry about that. This is going to be continuous learning and continuous understanding. But what's important is that we know when we get it wrong. We face into it, but it's going to happen."

I wholeheartedly agree with this and believe diversity is a journey, it's an evolutionary process, and we can use our platform, our power, for good to influence those CEOs and to hopefully drive this change in addition to government and other large institution. We will learn faster if we share our collective knowledge and we do not see each other as competitors, especially when it comes to diversity and inclusivity, and those future generations of leaders to come.

As I've mentioned previously, the ten holistic facets are a key part of understanding what true diversity and inclusion look like. I asked Steve Ingham why it's important for organisations to measure their employees through the lens of the facets. He replied:

Many people will relate to more than one of them, so it's a complicated area but we measure it, because if we don't know where we are, it's very difficult to make a difference. Measuring is a complicated process because a lot of these facets within themselves are hidden. A lot of people who suffer from mental health challenges or many other disabilities, they're going to work every day, hiding this disability. Now why would they do that? Are they going to fear that they won't be given the same opportunities, but they want to be respected in the same way as able-bodied colleagues? We have to be aware some people feel they can't talk openly about it, so we've got to be really careful about how we try to measure it.

We tried to be as accurate as possible, and, to do that, you've got to have those authentic messages from the leadership to reassure them that they can be open and honest. If they're constantly hearing from the leaders of that business how we believe in diversity and inclusion and all of these different ten facets, then they will gradually, I hope, feel more reassured to be honest and open about which facets they relate to and therefore what adaptations we can make, to make their life more comfortable in the workplace.

9

Where Are You Really From?

It's a very strange thing, being a minority member in the UK. As I told you when we embarked on this journey together, I was born in Hong Kong to Chinese parents who gave me up for adoption, so I was raised by White British parents, and lived in the UK for most of my life. While I could not be more grateful for the opportunity that afforded me, being of Chinese heritage in a White country has had a profound effect on me.

When we think about diversity in the UK – it's racial diversity that most people assume we're talking about. Now hopefully we can educate people to know that there are nine other facets of inclusion we should be looking at as well – but there's no question but that racial inequality is still a big part of the puzzle.

So let's start with our work at DIAL Global. Every year we produce the DIAL Global Diversity Review, examining how UK and US *organisations* are faring according to our metrics.

In 2023, looking at the facet of Race and Ethnicity, we identified the following. Five out of six UK companies say they have at least one member from a Black, South or East Asian or other minority ethnic background on their leadership team. That's 81%, up from 58% last year. A similar number say they include ethnic diversity in leadership succession planning (80%, up from 65%),

We reported that 2023 has seen a "sustained effort on race and ethnicity of many participating UK companies", with significantly more saying they have stated initiatives for increasing ethnic diversity in leadership (77%, up from 61%) and track progress against this (82%, up from 58%). Significantly more companies are also demonstrating to employees they are serious by ensuring senior leaders act as executive sponsors for their ethnic minority employee resource groups (78%, up from 59%).

In the US, ethnicity remains a key priority for organisations: 86% participants say they have at least one member from Black, Hispanic/Latino, South or East Asian, or other ethnic minority on their leadership team. Most of those surveyed include ethnic diversity in leadership succession planning (91%), however, monitoring the pay and progression of non-White employees has decreased significantly, with 72% saying they do this (down from 86% in 2022).

Some 92% of participating US companies have a Chief Diversity Officer, Head of Diversity and Inclusion, Diversity Director, or equivalent. Of those, only 27% report directly to the CEO, and the remainder (68%) report to a Human Resources function. Some 91% of participating US companies have a clear strategy for leadership team diversity. This has increased over 2022 when three in four respondents said they had a clear strategy (78%).

The key is not only to attract talent from all different backgrounds, but also retain them through their progression within the company. Our report stated:

> *Oftentimes, when Black, South or East Asian, Hispanic or other ethnic minorities are not developed in the same way as their White counterparts, intentionally or through unconscious bias, they leave the company, meaning the next generation of leaders does not include a pool of home-grown, ethnic minority talent. To combat this, 84% of UK companies we surveyed said they had dedicated outreach programs to recruit talent from Black, South or East Asian, Hispanic or other ethnic minority backgrounds, often in partnerships with universities, colleges and charities to recruit new, diverse talent early, as well as mentoring or sponsorship programs. Consciously changing recruitment practices is a key step in creating equity, but representation increases at the Leadership level will take more time.*

But, of course, while the work we do in helping organisations increase true diversity is crucial, in society we have much work to do.

I was so disappointed to read research in Spring 2023 from the University of Manchester, the University of St Andrews and King's College London which said more than a third of people from ethnic and religious minority groups in Britain have experienced some form of racist assault. The Evidence for Equality National Survey was carried out by the Centre on the Dynamics of Ethnicity, and reported the racism experienced ranged from physical, verbal, or damage to property and happened in all areas of life, including education, work, and when looking for housing.

Almost one in six respondents had experienced a racially motivated physical assault, but over a third of people identifying as Gypsy/Traveller, Roma or Other Black reported that they had been physically assaulted because of their ethnicity, race, colour, or religion.

Over a quarter had been verbally abused or insulted because of their ethnicity, race, colour, or religion, while nearly a third reported racial discrimination in education and employment.

Now this isn't necessarily going to be news to anyone who looks different in the UK.

At the end of 2020, the Equality and Human Rights Commission published a report on race inequality,[1] which demonstrated that the UK needed a distinct improvement in five areas, all of which are key to a happy, healthy, and secure life – employment, education, crime, living standard, and health & care.

In school, Black Caribbean and mixed White/Black Caribbean children had rates of permanent exclusion "about three times that of the pupil population as a whole".

The report also found unemployment rates were "significantly higher" for minority ethnic groups – 12.9% compared with 6.3% for white people. Black workers with degrees earned 23.1% less on average than White workers, while Black people who leave school with A-levels "typically got paid 14.3% less than their white peers". When it comes to promotion, a "significantly lower percentages of minority ethnic groups (8.8%) worked as managers, directors and senior officials, compared with 10.7% of white people".

Other key points of the report stated that "rates of prosecution and sentencing for black people were three times higher than for white people", and in England and Wales, children and adults from a minority ethnic background are more likely to be a victim of homicide.

This inequality seeps into home lives as well. The report stated that people from minority ethnic groups are more likely to live in poverty, with 35.7% of minority ethnic groups more likely to live in poverty compared with 17.2% of White people. Pakistani or Bangladeshi and Black adults are more likely to live in substandard accommodation than White people.

Sadly, this is very brief overview of some of the key points in the report. The full research makes grim reading. And let's not forget, this report focused on racial inequality – the reality for other groups struggling for equality is equally challenging.

As an adult, with the platform I now have, I have learned to be circumspect and pragmatic about what I can and can't change, but one of the hardest things I've found as I turned from being an awkward teenager trying to find myself into an adult woman of Chinese descent were the stereotypes I found myself the subject of. The ironic thing was, they were not just completely inaccurate and hurtful – they were entirely inconsistent.

I was approaching my identity through the prism of the outside world's expectations and understanding of my heritage – and it was an expectation and image which I knew was wrong and yet didn't know how to disentangle myself from it.

And it's hardly surprising. I remember stopping in my tracks when I heard about an interview on NPR with an academic talking about the hyper-sexualisation of East Asian women, and the often-overlooked intersection between racism and sexism.

Nancy Wang Yuen is Professor of Sociology at Biola University, California, and she was interviewed in the wake of a mass shooting in Atlanta, where eight people were killed, six of whom were East Asian women. The killer went on to blame his sex addiction.

In this interview, Wang Yuen talked about stereotypes attributed to East Asian women, telling the host, "I think submissive. I've actually been asked if my anatomy is different. So a kind of very fetishized, exoticized – that we're somehow even physiologically different from other women."

"Exotic lotus flowers", "dragon ladies", and "temptresses" were all stereotypes Wang Yuen, and the Chinese female host discussed. Wang Yuen said, "It's the kind of 'Madame Butterfly' or 'Miss Saigon' thing where you want them, but then you also can't have them. They're taboo. They're forbidden."

Referencing big Hollywood movies, they also looked at the sex worker image, accepting "The Asian prostitute is a very common stereotype". I was also fascinated and horrified in equal measure by the role US history played in creating stereotypes which went on to affect me. . .in little old Harrogate.

According to the interview: "The U.S. military had many wars with Asia, so there's a kind of thinking of Asia as a place that you want to take over, to dominate, and a fetishization of Asia proper as a country. When the GIs are over there, they're participating in the sex industry . . . and an association of being in Asia with sex workers, even though Asians are not any more likely to be sex workers than any other race or culture."

Lazy stereotype can have devasting effects. In 2021, Stop AAPI Hate found that in the 12 months prior, East Asian women made up 68% of the victims of anti-Asian hate crimes.

During the COVID-19 pandemic, against the backdrop of the rise in attacks on people of East Asian descent, I wrote an article about feeling like an outsider when growing up, due to the ignorance of those who knew little about Chinese culture.

I've included it here, because I think I will struggle to articulate the feelings I have as well as I did when writing through rage and tears in the wake of a surge of "Asian Hate" attacks.

As I mentioned in the piece, the fact COVID-19 had originated in China gave way to a torrent of abuse to anyone Chinese, or who looked Chinese to someone who knew no better. In 2021, an article in *The Independent* stated that "between January and June 2020, the Met Police recorded a total of 457 race-related crimes against people of 'Oriental' ethnicity or who self-defined as Chinese. In March alone the number was 101, nearly three times more than in March 2019 and 2018."

Despite my northern accent I still get enough questions about my heritage to make me feel "different". I'm proud to be British, however, I, like many others, feel conflict and cultural confusion – and it started when I was a child. I can still hear the casual jibes and the more deliberate racist remarks.

"What would happen if you had a Chinese mum and a Japanese dad?" the kids would ask, before taking their fingers up to their eyes and pulling them in different directions, laughing.

"Slitty eyes" and "Chink" I heard time and time again – as well as being told to "Go back to the takeaway."

A personal "favourite" is being told I'm "pretty for a Chinese woman". I've never figured out how I'm meant to take that.

My responses over the years have differed, depending on my life stage. In the early years, like most kids, I just wanted to fit in – so I was shy and embarrassed. I kept my head down. In my teens I adopted an eye-rolling superiority and used humour as a tool. But by the time I hit my 20s, I had years of pent-up anger and frustration, as well as a false sense of confidence, and my responses usually involved a "f**k you" type attitude.

I don't know if I will ever be able to explain to someone who has always fitted in what it feels like to be an imposter in your own skin. Trying to hide the shame of wanting to be a "proper" white westerner, and living up to the white, normalised standards of beauty, intelligence, popularity and respect I observed growing up.

Businesses in Chinatown were boycotted, and East Asian people bravely shared their accounts of abuse on social media. Labour MP Sarah Owen, who is half-Malaysian Chinese, told MPs in the House of Commons, "An undercurrent of anti-Asian racism has plagued this country well before the pandemic started, but now the lid has been lifted and the far-right have wrongly been given legitimacy to air their derision, violence and hatred."

When I addressed the issues of "Asian Hate" in my article mid-pandemic, I found unearthing those deep-rooted, long-overlooked, pushed-down emotions incredibly painful.

I found writing this cathartic and freeing – words which had been tangled up in my soul with nowhere to go finally found their place in my mind, my pen, and the world. I found it invigorating.

Then something else happened which had an extraordinary impact on society.

Revisiting the memories that have been buried for so many years is rather uncomfortable and brings back old trauma. Feelings of insignificance and wanting to be somewhat invisible. And, honestly, that's reinforced every time someone asks me that loaded question that anyone who's not 100% British knows all too well:

"Where are you *really* from?"

When I reassure whoever is asking that, yes, it's OK, I'm "really" from Harrogate, I feel the wave of acceptance – "Oh, right, you're not *really* Chinese." As if that makes me OK. When I was younger, I allowed this peculiar reassurance to actually make myself believe I was OK, and that I was accepted.

It reinforced my mindset of wanting to conform and wanting not to look so Chinese.

The added confusion for me, of course, is that I wasn't brought up in a Chinese home. I was adopted by a British couple, and while my mum and dad did a brilliant job of making sure I was taught about my Chinese heritage, it felt like something I learned, not something I was.

As I grew older, I became more attached to the vivid images which had been drawn for me. The energy, the colour, the philosophy, the meanings behind certain beliefs. The beauty of the Chinese Asian people, the hard work ethic, the ingenuity, the generosity, the entrepreneurialism.

In the main I now feel at peace with this duality in my life. But sadly the peace I have found within is yet to be established in the outside world.

The death of George Floyd.

On 25 May 2020, the 46-year-old died after being arrested by police outside a shop in Minneapolis, Minnesota. Footage of the arrest showed a police officer kneeling on Mr Floyd's neck while he was pinned to the floor, and transcripts of police bodycam footage later shows Mr Floyd said more than 20 times he could not breathe as he was restrained.

The world watched in horror, and all of a sudden business leaders realised they had a responsibility like never before.

Roz Brewer, now the former CEO of Walgreens Boots Alliance, said it was a wake-up call:

> *When the George Floyd incident happened I actually thought I knew it all, and I had been doing a good job in DE&I. And I quickly realised that even myself, who's been a huge proponent of it, myself who is a double minority, myself a mother of a young black male, I thought I understood this. But I realise that I didn't. I realise that I had not been asking all the right questions. I had not been focusing on the parts of our environment and our social environment that are very much broken.*
>
> *I think, myself included, we have been focusing on the D of DE&I and not equity and not inclusion. And I say that because what really happened with the George Floyd incident is that I don't think people understood the race issues that are happening in our country. Those that are left out and those who don't see a way out of their current situation.*

Carlos Cubia, EVP, Chief IED & Sustainability Officer at Corewell Health and former CDO at Walgreens Boots Alliance, told our publication, *Moving the DIAL*, about his experience on that dark day:

> *When George Floyd was murdered, we came into work the next day and some departments came in and started business as usual, like nothing had happened. But in my department I said to my leader, "I can't do this*

today, there was a man murdered on national TV last night." We just stopped everything, and had that discussion. And then I worked with the organisation to push that across the entire organisation and say, "You need to stop, take a moment, and give people an opportunity to breathe, because what just happened is, like, life-changing for all of us."

Many smart organisations realised how this horrific news story impacted its Black and minority ethnic workers and they had to be cared for. I will never forget watching Verizon CEO Hans Vestberg making a tearful and impassioned speech shortly after. He said:

Verizon is fiercely committed to diversity, inclusion across all spectrums, because it makes us, the world, a better place. I'm hopeful that the rest of the country will come to the understanding that valuing everyone equally is the best way forward. These events have really struck a chord for me and our entire leadership team. I know that many of you are deeply saddened and outraged by the events which have unfolded as well. I want our Black employees to know that they matter and they are valued. Although I don't share the same life experience, I want to listen, understand and I know that my leadership wants to do it as well.

For our employees, we're ensuring a safe place to share, discuss and gain the support they need during this particularly difficult time. For our society, I have directed our foundation to contribute 10 million US dollars to racial justice charities. The charities are the National Urban League, NAACP, National Action Network, Leadership Conference for Civil and Human Rights, Rainbow PUSH coalition and National Coalition of Black Civic Participation.

We will expand even more of our community-based effort to help and ensure we're making a difference where it matters. Our small part to help move the world forward. We have a responsibility as a large corporation to do right in these times. We cannot commit to brand purpose on moving the world forward unless we're committed to helping ensure we move forward for everyone.

I found this a staggeringly inspirational speech, not just what he said or the commitments he made, but the fact he was so visibly moved by the horrific events. I'm reminded of the quote I mentioned at the beginning of this book – that of Bank of America's CEO Brian Moynihan telling us, "Our jobs as CEOs now include driving what we think is right. It's not exactly political activism, but it is action on issues beyond business."

Hans really acted on issues beyond business and sums up the very essence of an Activist CEO.

Multiple times a year, at DIAL Global, we host a summit on a particular theme in the diversity space and we invite amazing guest speakers from around the world working in top-level roles in large organisations. Without fail, the murder of George Floyd has been mentioned in all of them, often in several sessions. The overwhelming sense was that this was a turning point for society, for race relations, and for employers to understand the devastating impact it had on their teams.

Misty Gaither, the Director & Global Head of Diversity Inclusion & Belonging for Indeed.Com, spoke so powerfully that I wanted to bring her words to you here:

> *The biggest change that I've experienced is the increase in acknowledgement around the lack of visible diversity of racial and ethnic minorities. I think vocalising that, people have been bold in calling it out in a way that we haven't experienced before. Because we have all been at home, we've seen this convergence of our backgrounds, we're in our homes and what that has helped with is the humanity that we get to see in our leaders and a kinder, more approachable, and vulnerable side that we don't typically see when we are hopping on airplanes or moving about our offices and in and out of meetings.*
>
> *I think there's been this acknowledgement and a calling out of aggression and microaggressions and fragility that we've all experienced at some part in our career, but we've been gaslit into thinking that it didn't really happen, that we might be a little bit crazy or convincing ourselves that we might be overreacting. All of this has come to the surface.*

She summed up the crisis point of COVID-19, George Floyd's murder, and the need for employers to step up, thus:

> *What can we do from a crisis response standpoint to actually whole-heartedly support all of our employees, whether it's our Black employee population, our parents and caregivers, our Asian-American, Pacific Islander communities. At the beginning of the pandemic we kept hearing that COVID-19 is a great equaliser but we quickly learned that was really false. So prior to George Floyd, we had some opportunities to say to our senior leaders, we have an issue and we need to understand that Black people are not okay. But we are forced to show up every day and pretend we can operate at the same capacity as everyone else. So let's start to have a conversation about that.*

One of the key takeaways from the death of George Floyd was the emotional impact the news footage had on people around the world, but of course in particular for people of colour. Imagine the impact of years of discrimination, micro aggressions, and exclusion.

Focusing on mental health in the workplace, the WHO tells us that a negative working environment can lead to physical and mental health problems.[2] Depression and anxiety have "a significant economic impact" with the estimated cost to the global economy of $1 trillion a year in lost productivity.

They report that harassment and bullying at work are commonly reported problems, and a "negative working environment may lead to physical and mental health problems, harmful use of substances or alcohol, absenteeism and lost productivity". They go on to tell us that "workplaces that promote mental health and support people with mental disorders are more likely to reduce absenteeism, increase productivity and benefit from associated economic gains".

In wider society we know that "being different" can have a profound affect on our mental health.

The charity Rethink states that if you are from a Black, Asian, or minority ethnic background, you "may experience different rates of mental illness than the white population. Things like fear, stigma and lack of culturally sensitive treatment can act as barriers to accessing mental health care for people from minority ethnic backgrounds."

The Mental Health Foundation states that Black men are more likely to have experienced a psychotic disorder than White men, and Black people are four times more likely to be detained under the Mental Health Act than White people, and older South Asian women are an at-risk group for suicide.

That's not to say people aren't sitting up and taking notice now.

In 2020, Citigroup's Chief Financial Officer, Mark Mason was the only Black executive among about 80 leaders atop the six biggest US banks. Since the murder of George Floyd, large banks have pledged to diversify their management and workforce.

UPS boss Carole Tomé is putting her money where her mouth is when it comes to racial equality in the workplace. "We know there is no place in any community anywhere in the world for racism, bigotry or hate," she said in one of her first public statements after becoming CEO. "We will not stand quietly or idly on the sidelines of this issue."

Charlene Thomas was made the newly created Chief Diversity, Equity and Inclusion Officer. The company also announced plans to invest more than $4 million in organisations that promote education, equity, and social justice.

"We didn't have the luxury of time because the world around us is changing so fast," she said, and has gone on to elevate the importance of diversity and inclusion. UPS also added five new board members – three women (one who is

Asian) and two Black men. UPS also is about roll out a new slogan: *You belong at UPS.*

"How inclusive is that?" Tomé announced.

Milena Mondini de Focatiis, Group Chief Executive Officer at Admiral has been doing excellent work in this sphere, including publishing their ethnicity pay gap data. In their most recent report,[3] she stated:

> One of the pillars our business was founded on 30 years ago was equality and we work hard to foster an inclusive workplace where everyone feels they can thrive and reach their full potential. I believe this is key to creating a more diverse workplace. I'm really proud that 94% of our colleagues believe that Admiral is a diverse and inclusive employer. For us, being a great place to work means prioritising an honest and transparent culture and I'm pleased that, for the first time, we can publish our ethnicity pay gap data. Over 80% of our colleagues have chosen to share their ethnicity data with us. Our figures reflect the fact that we have a higher proportion of colleagues from ethnically diverse backgrounds working in functions which attract higher salaries, such as IT, Data, Finance and Technology. We're committed to ensuring that all of our teams represent the customers and communities which we serve.

Find Your Voice, Find Your Mentors

I recently interviewed Leena Nair, now the CEO of Chanel, for one of our DIAL Global Summits and while she was at Unilever at the time, I find myself now coming back to her words because her leadership style hinges on making life better for other people – another example of true CEO Activism:

> It's been a privilege and burden of my life to be the first woman at everything I've done in my career in the last 28 years. That has meant it has brought a heightened sense of responsibility for me. One of the first

things that helped me find my voice was to think that I was not doing it for myself, but I was doing it in the service of others I was doing it to make things easier for others who came after me.

You've got to find your voice because you're constantly thinking about those who come after you. I've got this huge platform and responsibility. How do I make it easier? It's not easy. You need to find mentors, because the power and influence came much later in my career, but early on the pressure to conform was as high on me as on anybody else. You want to conform. You want to be like the majority. You don't want to be unique and standing out, you don't want to be differentiated. And it's scary when you walk into a room and you're constantly the only "only" in the room. You feel heightened expectation, heightened pressure on you, heightened visibility, everything you do, your successes are amplified, your failures are doubly amplified. So it does take a bit of mentorship and support and peer support to be able to find your voice when you find yourself in a minority.

She also told us, leadership and influence can be a numbers game:

In 500 leaders I need to influence, about a third of them are never going to get it, so I'm not going to waste my time on them. Another third is on the fence – they will blow whichever way they think the wind is blowing. And the third are genuine champions. Find those genuine champions who are waiting to help.

Leverage your own voice to make the change that you need to really want.

Gavin Lewis, Managing Director at Black Rock, appeared on my podcast only weeks after the death of George Floyd:

When I first started talking about the subject of racial diversity in the finance industry or asset management industry, I couldn't point to many other people like me, certainly no one above me and I think that's still the case. Certainly no one next to me, and few people behind me.

It does feel though that over the last 23 years, there has been a greater influx of black professionals into the industry, which I think is a sign of progression. But I also have to realise that when it comes to my own experience, my own background, it's still a rarity, particularly at senior level. I grew up in Tottenham in a single-parent family on a council estate in Tottenham.

I realise I'm a role model, a reluctant role model, but I do spend a lot of time and exert a lot of energy trying to change the fortunes for other people.

When I entered the industry I would go to conferences and be the only black person in the room full of thousands of people, and I'd get mistaken for the help or someone serving drinks. But I didn't let it deter me – not because I have this inner steel but because I got used to being kind of the odd one out, so then when you overlay that with some resilience, that helps.

What I'm trying to do now is ensure that it's easier for people who are entering the industry now but I'm also trying to make life easier for myself. Because when I speak to young people, they may face a lot of challenges in the workplace, and then they will look at someone who's senior and think "you've made it", but they don't know that, well, I still face the same challenges. And maybe if I talk about it, and I'm vocal about it and I'm asked about it, I can change my own experience as well.

These words really struck a chord with me. One can be a leader, an Activist CEO, but still find ourselves fighting for our own place at the top table. I think it's very easy for individuals to think if "you've made it", you don't suffer with these things. I would argue, as a CEO, it's something that still can happen day in and day out. And, occasionally, I even find it catches me off guard when I'm not expecting it. One can have a hard outer shell and can easily take knocks but discrimination can still catch you off guard. The people who pave the way need support – I've been in boardrooms before and I've been the only female and Asian person there – and it's isolating.

Gavin agreed with me, and noted an uptick in interest in his diversity work after George Floyd's death, but that it didn't last once the headlines moved on.

We've been screaming. We've been screaming and no sound is coming out. It's loud to us, but no one's hearing it. Silence. There are firms who really have made this a priority and I think that's excellent. But I don't think there's a sweeping change has happened yet. It might have felt like it. But when I look at the number of people that said "we want to do this" and suddenly it's gone very, very quiet.

Entrepreneurship

So far we've examined this facet through the lens of large organisations, but what does the picture look like when it comes to minority ethnic groups taking the plunge and setting up on their own?

In 2022, more than a third of ethnic minority business owners reported making no profit in 2021, compared with 15% of white, female business owners, while 49% of ethnic minority entrepreneurs cite difficulties getting finance as the reason why they stopped work on their business idea.

In the summer of 2023, I saw an article on the BBC about funding from VCs for female- or minority-led businesses. The headline stated that, according to MPs, "Britain's venture capital industry is failing to invest in companies started by women and minority ethnic entrepreneurs."

The Treasury Committee was told firms with all-female founders received only 2% of venture capital funding in 2021, with even less investment going to firms led by minority ethnic executives.

Yet, in the autumn of 2023, the Lending Standards Board revealed their new report found ethnic minority entrepreneurs contribute an estimated £25bn to the UK economy.[4]

This reminded me of a conversation I had with Bina Mehta, the Chair of KPMG, on just this issue, when DIAL launched. She told me, back in 2020:

> *We're seeing an increased proportion of businesses that are either wholly run by females or partly, and similarly with ethnically diverse leaders as well. I've been involved in a number of things that we've done around the Asians in Tech Entrepreneurship programme to help these entrepreneurs. A lot of the time it's not that they don't have access to things, sometimes it's just joining the dots for people.*
>
> *What I've seen is an incredible growth in what I call technology entrepreneurs, and it's really, really exciting and it's really, really inspiring. I would say the third generations of Asians are very, very focused on either [traditional roles] or entrepreneurship in its entirety. There will be a small proportion of entrepreneurs who just want to maintain the business a certain size and run it, but most of them will have ambitions right away to grow.*
>
> *Investors are putting the onus on themselves to be more cognisant of the fact that their portfolios have to be more diverse.*
>
> *How do we help underrepresented entrepreneurs? How do we make sure that the people that deploy those funds are deploying them in an unbiased way?*

The Activist CEOs

Whenever we wrap up one of our DIAL Global summits, I can guarantee that two people in particular that viewers will say have made the biggest impact will be Ray Dempsey and Carlos Cubia.

Ray is the Group CDO at Barclays, where he joined after 22 years working his way up the ranks at BP. This journey came to him after 7 years as an engineer, and he's been named by *Savoy* magazine as one of the Most Influential Black Executives in Corporate America three times. Here's his story:

I grew up in a US military family, I'm an Army brat. So, from a young age, I found myself always turning up in new places, new schools, and new friends, I lived all over the US and even spent a few years in Germany. And I know that that created in me an instinct and appetite to learn about difference, to learn about different people, to try to understand what it is that drives and motivates people in different settings and different contexts.

In some ways, it was probably about trying to make sure I knew who to avoid, so I didn't get beat up, and who to make friends with so that I found myself in the best circumstances in all those new places.

But the truth is that those instincts really carried me into my professional life. I've lived in 12 homes at BP, so, again, a really rapid pace of moving house and finding new friends, new communities, and learning about different places. At the time, it was all great training for me to step into a role leading diversity, equity, and inclusion.

With a business background, I find that I speak the language of business leaders, I am deeply reliant on data and insights to help point out where the gaps are, and ask what is it that we need to do to close them, and then to apply practical and pragmatic approaches to delivering on that. I think my ability to engage business leaders as partners in doing those things is a real consequence of having lived and worked and applied my experience and ideas in so many different places.

My life has been an experiment in diversity, equity, and inclusion.

And that's why it has now very much become not just my job, but my mission, my purpose.

This is hard work. And it does require a lot of perseverance and sometimes it can be lonely, because everyone is busy focused on their priorities. They're part of the business or their function. And sometimes this DEI feels like it's an add-on. It's a really important part of the way we go about this work to make sure everyone feels that it's for all of us. And there's a part for all of us to play. But along the way, there are plenty of moments where it's just a few of us pushing this big rock up what feels like quite a pointy hill. There are also lots of great days where we know there's lots of others joined in with this, and they're helping to push that rock and sometimes even the hill doesn't feel quite so steep. So that's what keeps us optimistic and keeps us motivated towards the end.

When I joined Barclays two years ago, there was already a fantastic foundation of this work that engaged across communities. There were seven at the time and Barclays was still calling them networks, and network is not a bad word. Lots of companies and organisations still use that language. But I saw an opportunity to expand the understanding and the appreciation of what can be contributed to these communities by moving through that evolution from networks to what we now describe as ERGs [Employee Resource Groups].

We've expanded now to a set of 12. There is so much energy and passion within our colleagues based around the work of the ERGs. There are some 25,000 colleagues worldwide that are involved, and that's out of 85,000 colleagues in the whole company around the world, so it's a really high proportion. And they don't just follow along, they don't just get together occasionally and share celebrations. They have contributed to the bank in real ways. Our black professionals resource group work together to create a development programme, particularly for young black professionals in the bank.

I'm just really delighted by what I see. We rely on our ERGs to really lead the way through the big celebrations, whether it's Asian Pacific Heritage Month or Hispanic Heritage Month in the US or Pride Month or any of the other celebrations. It's really their own ideas and initiative and the framing of the right subjects, the right guests in the right way to engage broadly around the bank. It's fun to watch. And it's making a real difference.

Too often, even from a young age, we're conditioned to believe that what we should do to be on a pathway of success is find a way to fit in. And actually what the world needs are people who are prepared to go off the path, to create new ideas, to push for new possibilities, and to say what they really think and to be courageous, take risks, take chances, and try to cause things to happen that haven't happened before.

Carlos Cubia echoes many of these pearls of wisdom. He's former Walgreens Boots Alliance SVP and Global

Chief Diversity, Equity and Inclusion Officer – and puts that same authenticity at the heart of what he does. He stated:

I've always moved to the beat of a different drum. When I was growing up in Pontiac, Michigan, my friends would follow the crowd, and while I was part of the crowd, I did my own thing. So that lesson to me is you can still be yourself and be accepted. You just have to be your true authentic self.

It's nothing I learned – it's just how I was going to move through life. When I was in high school, I was on a track team, but I wasn't your typical sprinter. I was a pole vaulter. I didn't know any other African Americans that did pole vaulting! I don't know that I was a person that tried to break down barriers or to walk differently. I just did it by choice.

You knew you had to prepare yourself for what was out there because we knew things weren't equal, we had to work harder, and we had to do more. For African American kids coming up in Pontiac, we really had to create opportunities for ourselves.

There have been a number of bosses throughout my career that have had a major impact on me, but the most impactful has been my most recent boss at Walgreens Boots Alliance, Kathleen Wilson Thompson. She was the Global Chief Human Resources Office and a champion for D & I. She was a huge supporter and proponent of this work, and of me, personally. She just had a cool head, stayed humble, and never let any of that shape who she was. To talk to her you would never know that she has the success that she has garnered over the years. She would always say: "God gave you a voice and you have to use it for good."

At WBA, I get to do very fulfilling work, very interesting work, and work that is very meaningful and necessary in today's environment. But it presents a challenge every single day, because, regardless of how you present it and no matter what the data and information you show to some individuals, they're going to see this work differently. They're going to see this work as taking something away from them, giving an advantage to somebody else that maybe they don't feel deserve it or they feel like it's unfair.

If we try to create equitable situations where other people can have the same chance, others may say, "Well, if you're giving them something, you should be giving me the same", even though they've already attained something. That's the conflict that I have in this work.

There's a lot of expectation. People think you have all the answers, and that you can solve the problems just by the nature of your title in the role that you're in. The burden shouldn't be mine to bear alone, or my team or anyone else that's doing this kind of work. This is really a collective effort for everyone.

When George Floyd was murdered, we came into work the next day and some departments came in and started business as usual, like nothing had happened. But in my department I said to my leader, "I can't do this today, there was a man murdered on national TV last night." We just stopped everything, and had that discussion. And then I worked with the organisation to push that across the entire organisation and say, "You need to stop, take a moment, and give people an opportunity to breathe, because what just happened is, like, life-changing for all of us."

I would not say we're in a better place. What I will say we're in a different place – because we are now allowing those conversations to happen in the workplace where two and a half years ago, those were taboo. Your workforce is a microcosm of society. There are differences that exist within our workforce, we have to value and respect those differences. We have to understand what our company values are. What's our vision and our purpose as an organisation, and this is the piece where I come in. If you're going to represent our organisation and be a part of it, this is the expectation of you.

Notes

1. www.equalityhumanrights.com/our-work/our
2. www.who.int/.../detail/mental-health-at-work
3. admiralgroup.co.uk/ethnicity-pay-gap-report-2023
4. www.lendingstandardsboard.org.uk/unlocking

10

A Billion Strong

Over a billion people around the world have some form of disability. A billion. And yet so many are left to flounder in the workforce – either being overlooked for employment or not given the tools to thrive.

In our most recent DIAL Global Diversity Review, we found 88% of participating UK companies say they encourage honest discussions around disability in the workplace. Of the UK companies surveyed, close to all organisations support their disabled staff with the most vital aspects to do their jobs, with 92% offering workplace adjustments and 93% having employee assistance lines or occupational health services geared towards employees with disabilities.

Some 72% provide further support in the form of mentoring, coaching, or buddying for employees with disabilities (up from 47% last year). And 66% train and equip staff and line managers with specific training around disability, with many others saying they do so "on requirement" as the need arises (up 39% over 2022).

As the brilliant Ramcess Jean-Louis, Global Chief Diversity, Equity and Inclusion Officer of Pfizer said:

Our work with Diversity, Equity and Inclusion is constantly evolving. As we become more educated on the lived experiences of different underserved communities, we must challenge ourselves to do more and adapt to truly meet their needs. When it comes to the disability community – one of the most overlooked and marginalised groups – we have seen significant evolution in the language and terminology used to describe the community, the education on disability inclusion, and the support the community receives.

At Pfizer, we understand that disability is a part of a person's identity that should be recognised and embraced. When colleagues have access to the tools and technologies they need, as well as an inclusive and empowering work environment, everyone thrives. People need to feel safe to bring their whole selves to work. They need to trust the company and their colleagues, so they don't feel they need to hide any part of their identity, including their visible or invisible disability. We believe every person deserves to be seen, heard, and cared for just as they are. At Pfizer, we are intentional in nurturing this trust and we strive to enhance and innovate our support for disabled and neurodivergent colleagues.

Although still performing in the bottom half of our ten facets, disability and neurodiversity have seen a significant improvement overall, now with an index score of 74, compared to 62 in 2022. This is largely due to companies moving beyond the core requirements of offering workplace adjustments, and providing disabled and neurodivergent staff with more holistic support. More companies now say they have created mentoring, coaching, or buddying programmes, and a significant higher number are training line managers on how to best support those with disabilities.

While companies must, and do, comply with providing workplace adjustments, fewer actively look past invisible disabilities and those who are neurodivergent. Only two in five say they have digital accessibility policies, suggesting this is often under the radar. From our own member community, we know that avant-garde organisations include both disabilities and neurodivergence in their self-ID campaigns, logging these within HR systems and providing bespoke support as required.

Of the UK companies we interviewed who were focusing on disability, all said they enlisted the help of the community and/or experts to first gain an understanding of the many complex issues involved. Some started with asking employees with disabilities to share experiences and workshop the most effective strategies required for a more inclusive workplace, while others enlisted the help of dedicated organisations to help them navigate the many potential pitfalls.

It's a slightly different picture in the US as 75% of participating US companies say they encourage honest discussions around disability in the workplace. Almost all organisations support their disabled staff with the most vital aspects to do their jobs, with 90% offering workplace adjustments and 78% having employee assistance lines or occupational health services geared towards employees with disabilities.

Some 77% provide further support in the form of mentoring, coaching, or buddying for employees with disabilities (up from 51% last year). And 73% train and equip staff and line managers with specific training around disability, with many others saying they do so "on requirement" as the need arises (up 43% over 2022).

> Continuing its performance in the bottom half of our ten facets, disability and neurodiversity have seen some progress in terms of support for colleagues who are differently abled, but no significant improvements have been made with regards to companies actively looking to hire more and promote staff with disabilities. Where there has been progress, it relates to more companies now stating they have created mentoring, coaching or buddying programmes (77%, up 26%), and a significant higher number are training line managers on how to best support those with disabilities (73%, up 30%).

So let's look at how the climate has changed over the last few years.

There are some incredible CEO Activists leading the charge. I'm continually impressed by the Valuable 500 – the 500 CEOs uniting their organisations to form a global business network working together to end disability exclusion.

Similarly, the Disability:IN CEO Letter on Disability Inclusions moved me greatly. Some 180 CEOs signed an open letter in order to show they're "taking action to build inclusive, accessible and equitable workplaces".

Julie Sweet, Chair and CEO of Accenture, commented: "At Accenture, accelerating disability inclusion is key to our commitment to creating a culture of equality where everyone can advance and thrive, and core to our strategy of being an innovation-led company."

In their open letter they wrote:

> *Understanding that we are all operating in an unprecedented environment with multiple, competing interests for the time and attention of the CEO, we are writing to you – from a CEO to CEO perspective – to ask for your much-needed help in advancing equality and inclusion at a time when the need to make sure that no one is marginalized has never been more important.*
>
> *July 2020 marked the 30th Anniversary of the Americans with Disabilities Act (ADA). While there is much to celebrate in the progress that has been made since the ADA was created, there is still a great deal of work to be done.*

They went on to specifically request participation in the Disability Equality Index (DEI), the corporate benchmarking tool for disability equality, that important information on disability inclusion that details its impact on business performance is shared, and that organisations are aware of "increasing investor interest in understanding how companies are inclusive of people with disabilities".

And this was the stand-out moment for me when they wrote:

> *We have experienced first-hand, within our companies, the potential for innovation, sustainability, and profit as a result of disability inclusion. It is important to us, now more than ever, to drive companies aligned with corporate values and meaningful purpose. Without disability inclusion, we will fail to build sustainable futures that empower all.*
>
> *We understand, first-hand, that many requests come across the CEO's desk, which is why we're reaching out directly to you on this topic. The business case for disability inclusion in the workplace is compelling. Investor interest – along with regulator and legislator interest – on the topic of workplace disability inclusion is increasing at an accelerated pace.*

And the DEI provides an unbiased and confidential way to benchmark disability inclusion in the workplace.

Wow. Just wow.

I loved not just the wording and intent of this open letter but that it was an example of CEO Activists empowering others by working together and showing that a new gold standard in business practice has arrived. It clearly demonstrated that it's imperative for twenty-first-century leaders to take a stand and make fundamental changes.

There was another story I came across recently which really reminded me that, actually, a lot of this is really quite simple. Grant Beckett, Head of Corporate Strategy at WorkHuman, was on a business trip to Germany when he was in a horrific car accident which left him with life-changing injuries. When he woke up in hospital, he told the *Boston Globe*, he opened his eyes to the vision of his wife. . . .and his CEO Eric Mosley – who also sorted out flights for his wife, organised childcare and collected his dog. "In a crisis like this, I knew it was important to just be there for Grant and his family," said Mosley modestly.

At the DIAL Global Summits, we dig deep on all the issues that affect our workforce, but some of the events where I leave feeling like we really made a difference were the sessions around disability and inclusion. We have had some incredible speakers at these events, such as Steve Ingham – the CEO of the Michael Page Group, who was paralysed after an accident and who's shared his unique experience of being a leader with two very different lived experiences.

And then, of course, LaMondre Pough and Debra Ru – the Founders of Billion Strong, a disability movement dedicated to the education, the unity, and the elevation of the global community of people with disabilities. If there is ever anyone I want fighting my corner, it's this powerhouse. Pough told DIAL Global:

> *Despite hearing about the advantages that people with disabilities can offer employers, too many companies still hold themselves back when it comes to hiring people with disabilities. They see hiring some persons with disabilities as being the right thing to do, but do not see it as a part of the talent strategy that will benefit the company and outweigh what they see as potential complications, expenses and risks.*
>
> *Now, that mindset puts companies at a disadvantage when it comes to acquiring and leveraging the talent they need in today's tight job market. However, many leaders are changing these outdated mindsets and forging new paths for talent management and reaping the rewards of it.*
>
> *I am a person with a visible disability and I have lived experiences as a person with a disability. The reason that I am so passionate about the disability community, and society as a whole, is because I'm a person who believes that we all can make the world a better place, and this is a part of what I can do to make the world a better place.*
>
> *Inclusive environments, environments where people belong, environments where people feel like they are truly a part of it, is how we make this world a better place. And that's why I'm so passionate about it.*
>
> *We are getting to a point now where people are starting to recognise more than the disability. So often when we start to have this disability conversation, it becomes the overarching theme of that individual to the point where they are truly defined by disability. My disability is not the defining point. It is a defining point of who I am, but it's certainly not the defining point. Just like I'm a black man. I'm a black man raised in the South of the United States. That certainly does shape my perspective of the world, but it is not the only thing that shapes the perspective. I often say because of COVID-19, because of the pandemic, instead of this work-life balance, we had a work-life collision, and so all of these things have to come to the table now. It's becoming more widely accepted that now we are complete people, we are whole people. All of us are bringing all of who we are to the table.*

Paulette Cohen is Head of Diversity and Inclusion for Barclays in the UK and Europe – and I've had the honour of working with her on many events at DIAL. One of the things that always fascinated me has been her background in the charity sector. I remember at one of our events her telling me "you can take the girl out of the charity, but so everything I do is driven by a sense of social purpose".

This is one of many reasons why Paulette falls into the category of CEO Activist in my eyes. "I've had the privilege at Barclays to learn so much from my colleagues of all abilities from their lived experience. I'd like to think that I'm an ally that learns from and supports them." She continued:

> It's important to recognise that all abilities count, and to actually consider the talents that colleagues with the disability, mental health or neurodiverse conditions can actually bring to the business. And that's both the professional skills that they bring, but also additional talents like exceptional resilience or adaptability. It also enables us to better understand our customers.
>
> And the second principle that I've come to love in this space is about future-proofing opportunity. I talk about future-proofing rather than retrofitting. I know that's in particular around accessibility issues, but also development opportunities. It's building in things up to start, not thinking about things somewhere down the line as an afterthought.
>
> Barclays is a Disability Confident leader – a status now that's particularly pertinent to the UK, where the UK Department of Work and Pensions has a scheme called Disability Confidence and it is designed to help businesses and other organisations to find ways to recruit disabled talent into that organisation.
>
> It enables us to actively seek disabled talent. And to do that, we've adapted some of our processes – we've adapted some of our recruitment processes, some of our assessment processes. We launched an initiative called Able to Enable, which was a bespoke apprenticeship scheme that made sure we didn't just use the standard system, but we looked at the whole recruitment process through the lens of colleagues with a disability or mental health condition. And that really enabled us to bring some extraordinary people into the business who otherwise might not have had that opportunity.

But once you have talent within the business, there's something really important about making sure that the environment is right to retain and to follow up that talent.

There is still a huge fear factor there of the unknown. People are afraid of what they don't know. We need to connect with disability organisations. We need to kind of build those relationships stronger, to have people with disabilities feeding into our companies in terms of employment.

But the fear, the fear isn't just necessarily by the company owners. It can be other employees within the organisation because they may not know, they may have preconceptions about, how do I talk to somebody with a disability? What if I say the wrong thing? How do I work?

It's also fear on the part of the person with the disability. As organisations, not many of us are doing a really good job to say that we are. We are organisations that respect and love equality, and when you come into our organisation, you'll be treated with respect, you'll be treated equally.

You will have the same opportunities for advancement as any anybody else.

Companies need to look at the end-to-end experience of somebody with a disability coming in, and that starts at the recruitment stage, not when they're in the door on day one. How are things advertised? How are they written? Is there reasonable accommodation for interviews? How do you hope to get people even in the door?

What are people's onboarding like when they're in the organisation? Do smaller organisations need support from government in terms of providing those reasonable accommodations if they do cost money? But in many, many cases they don't. It could be flexible working hours.

This does not have to be overly complicated. Talk to your people, talk to your employees, train them.

If we go in with an open mind and try and figure this out together, we'll get there. We will get there.

Vivian Ayuso-Sánchez is another leader, though while not a CEO, I would certainly attribute the term 'activist' to her. I interviewed her when she was the Senior Manager of the Diversity Networks & Programs at Walgreens and remain ever impressed.

We invited her to speak at one of our DIAL Global summits and her words really stayed with me. She said:

I have always believed from a very young age about the fundamental right of people, of all people, to be treated fairly, equally and equitably. This applies to my personal as well as my professional life. I moved to the US at a fairly young age, part of a minority population where English was my second language. It all leads to a true awareness and deep passion for all aspects of diversity, equity, and inclusion. And how fortunate for me that the bulk of my career has been precisely in this field.

There are some really exciting changes that have happened in the last number of years. The conversation on disability now permeates all levels in the companies. Companies have shown a renewed focus and stronger than ever in the last couple of years when it comes to diversity and inclusion.

But to truly value diversity, we must include people with disabilities in that definition. We cannot forget this group, that they represent the largest minority group in the world, and it cuts through all races, ethnicities, and genders. Why would we not tap into this community?

We have been offering a placement programme that allows people to go through a training and at the end of the training programme they're guaranteed placement. It has created an environment and a culture that are completely and totally accepting of people with disabilities. And these individuals are identifying and coming forward in a way like we don't see anywhere else. Our percentage is extremely high and it's just the culture that we want to emulate throughout.

The pandemic helped create environments and opportunities that ended up benefiting many of us and clearly benefiting people with disability. These include the flexibility on our work, how work is done, where we do work and when we do work. Improved use of reasonable accommodations and accessibility tools. We have become so much better providing closed captioning and providing ASL translators as needed, something that perhaps many of us were not focusing on before. We're offering more part-time opportunities and work-sharing opportunities that again benefit all but we have seen some of our programmes provide great benefit for people with disabilities.

We've addressed subjects like deafness, autism, multiple sclerosis, epilepsy, cancer, mental health and more.

Leadership is talking about this more than ever, and this is really exciting to see – like the Valuable 500 CEOs publicly committing to disability inclusion and accessible ability. And I'm proud to say our own CEO at WBA, Roz Brewer, is one of those CEOs that has done this. Companies are also using the Disability Equality Index or similar tools in the US and abroad to benchmark our performance in relation to disability in the workplace and identify areas for improvement. And these tools are critical as we work with intentionality to improve our offerings in this space.

As I've been gathering my thoughts around Activist CEOs, I realise they fall into two categories: the ones who are driven by listening to others' lived experiences, and the ones who have their own exceptional stories.

I've been fortunate enough, as I'm sure you are learning as you go on this journey with me, to work with incredible people at the Co-op. Helen Webb, OBE, is the Chief People Officer at WH Smith's and the former Chief People and Services Officer of the Co-op. She shared:

I think my passion was born at a very young age. I have an older brother who was born without arms. He was my big brother and I knew no different as a kid, but what I saw is how he has thought through his life, how my parents fought for him when he couldn't fight for himself, to create actual equity in the chances and opportunities that he had.

I'm incredibly proud of him. He's a professor of astrophysics. He's got a brain the size of the planet. He's got a lovely family, I've got lovely nephews, and there's nothing that he can't or won't try to do. So, for example, when he was at school, he loved rugby. He loved watching rugby but couldn't play. So he went to his teachers and said, "Well, can I be a referee?" So he trained to be a referee.

But lots of people haven't got that. They haven't got that opportunity. They haven't got somebody actually speaking up for them. And I believe that that's my job, that's my role. That's what I've done throughout my career. And it's really important because unless you create a system within your organisation that is inclusive, you're genuinely missing out on huge talent.

I'm really lucky because we formed a new networking group called REPRESENT. They asked me if I would be the executive sponsor of the networking group, which I was very privileged to do. Some of the work that we've already begun is having a huge impact because, in launching the group, we brought to life some really personal stories of why simple adjustments and some real focus could actually create a big difference.

I did an interview with a store manager who's partially sighted – he told me how some simple lighting equipment and some simple IT software would mean that his job was so much easier. He's an amazing leader and we want him to have those opportunities, so what my blog did was allow the IT team to come to the table and they said, "What can we do to help?"

We've got sponsors now in our IT team to make sure that from a reasonable adjustment perspective, we have explored all avenues and we have got the equipment, and we've got the equipment to the right people at the right time.

I think the networks are incredibly important because you have to have the conversation about lived experiences because any one team in the organisation has not got all the answers. To create an inclusive environment, you have to listen to your people. You have to make sure that whatever listening you're doing is from a broad section of the population that you employ as much as possible. And, interestingly, we've had an example of intersectionality because the groups do talk, the networking groups do talk to each other, but our group for disabled colleagues and Aspire, which is our women's group, have been talking to each other recently about how they share experiences and how in a sense they mentor each other about the issues, and how they make sure that the issues represented by disabled women are actually covered through both networks.

What we've discovered from our disabled colleagues is that the commute to work is often prohibitive. You have to get to work and public transport isn't always the best. And you talk to our women's work group and again the commute is often prohibitive because of childcare and the hours at each end of the day. So actually having that conversation about how we work in a hybrid environment going forwards, there are very similar issues. The elongation of the day because of the commute actually can be prohibitive for disabled colleagues and for women.

As I've stressed many times, I am a huge believer in intersectionality and how we can bring all those individual, diverse parts of ourselves to align with the individual, diverse parts of others. It's one of the reasons I've been so passionate about the DIAL Global Diversity Review in the UK and the US, and I was delighted to work with Evelyn Aspinall, the Global EDC Officer for Unilever, on the report. Evelyn told me:

> *I'm Brooklyn-born and raised, from immigrant parents from Honduras in Central America. After college, I worked in consulting, but at the end of the day, every issue that we dealt with had to do with diversity. It had to do with people interacting with each other and how you get inclusion.*
>
> *Very early on in my career, someone said to me, "Don't define yourself by your title." If you don't have a mentor in the company, find a mentor somewhere else and look for what you want to learn and not a role that you want to get. Well, I just had ten years with Unilever and I had no clue that that would happen, but I think it's an organisation that understands how to nurture creativity, how to foster leadership, and how to give people a real line of sight to how their purpose can be manifested and work through in the company.*
>
> *I'm the only Latina at Vice President level. And so why is that relevant? We're in 150 company countries. We have 500 brands every day; 3 billion people use our products. And when you look at the top of the house, we've been working very hard to have gender parity at management and above. We hit 50/50 gender balance in 2019, a year ahead of schedule.*
>
> *But when you peel the onion and you look at that top layer, the pyramid is still there and the female population becomes whiter, European, and older. And so we were still trying to now get 50/50 at each level. And when you are in an intersectional world, you can't help but represent.*
>
> *I'm seen as a role model by other Latinas in the US, in other parts of the world. I've worked in Mexico, so Latin America sees me as a role model. I'm a mother and I'm married, so all of these things come together.*

I have a disability, I have dyslexia and ADHD, which I think is my superpower, not a disability actually, but what the company's been able to do that allowed me to choose to stay was give me a sense of purpose. I know what my personal purpose is and I can see how I can use my role to achieve it.

As someone who has dyslexia myself, I've always been particularly conscious of how it's affected me, my work, my self-confidence and, of course, what CEOs are doing to address it for their employees. Martin McKay, CEO and founder of Text Help, is someone I've explored a shared background with. He stated:

We are a technology company, software company, and we make software tools for people with dyslexia and people who have difficulty with literacy and actually math and schools as well. A good part of our business is in education, but a growing and important part of our business is in workplace and we're trying to provide tools for employers so that they can support neurodiverse employees, like employees with dyslexia.

When I was about 12 years old, my dad had a stroke and he lost the ability to use his right arm and right leg and he lost his ability to speak. He couldn't really read or write or communicate very well and he used to be a teacher. He was always a very articulate and driven person, and him losing the ability to do all those things had a big impact on me. I was young and when I was old enough, I started to make tools, software, things to help people communicate. I started out for people with strokes, motor neuron disease, and cerebral palsy.

I was talking to a lady in Scotland who told me that she had one student with cerebral palsy and about 200 students with dyslexia. And if I could do something to help dyslexic students, I could really reach a lot more people. And I didn't really understand dyslexia at that time, but I did some research. I actually ended up flying to California to meet a guy called Marshall Raskin who had done a study on spelling disorders and was a specialist in dyslexia and learning difficulties. He shared his research with me and that helped me write our first dyslexic spell checker.

We've reached 50 million students in education alone around the world. We've got offices in Oslo and Malmo and our US headquarters is in Boston. We've got about 100 staff here in the US with 350 staff around the world. It's grown into quite a big business.

My glasses are my assistive technology, so it's just the same way for dyslexic people. In schools in the US, for example, 12% of kids are in special education, so they'll have dyslexia, they'll be on the autism spectrum, have physical disabilities or visual impairment. When they leave school, they don't leave their dyslexia behind or their autism behind. They take it with them into the workforce. And in school we have special education and we need to make work special. We need to make sure that HR departments are aware that 8% of their employees are probably dyslexic and they won't put their hand up and say, "Hey, I'm dyslexic."

Should we either not ask the question or look at putting in interventions and have workforces talk about this proactively and openly, that allow the creation of a space, a safe space internally. that says we're proud of our differences, we're proud of our employees thinking differently?

Diane Lightfoot is the CEO of the Business Disability Forum. When I interviewed her, I remember being so inspired by just how much of a vocation inclusion in the disability space is for her. Diane stated:

I'm absolutely passionate about the role of good work in transforming people's lives and in the context of people with learning disabilities. I think it's, in a way, the most complete form of inclusion that there is.

I get to work with just fabulous, committed people who are so passionate about disability inclusion and then to go out to our 300-plus members and partners and they collectively employ about 20% of the UK workforce, so there's a big impact there. We work with them in a really practical way to help them to support their disabled employees, to recruit additional disabled employees. It's this really kind of practical intervention and practical support that we can provide that in lots of cases makes a difference between somebody keeping their job or not, which is fantastic, and then progressing.

On the other side of the same coin is that because we work with this huge wealth of employers across all sectors, we then have this brilliant evidence base that we can then feed into, into policy, and into government, and really show again practically what does work for an employer and what does work for business to help shape future policy. That's why we were set up in the first place – to make sure that a new policy at the time, the Disability Discrimination Act ,wasn't just a lovely set of intentions, but that it was actually able to be operationalised and practical for businesses to be able to do. And that's still what we exist to do.

When it comes to my own career plan, I used to think whatever level I was going for next, "Maybe this is massively jumped up of me to think I could be a manager, a director, certainly a CEO." I have worried about telling people that I was going to search for these jobs in case they thought, "Bless, that's nice that she thinks she can do this, but it's a bit ridiculous." So I'd like to say to my younger self, believe in yourself. And also that most people feel the same. The amount of people that I talk to who've got new CEO roles or senior roles who say, "Gosh, I feel like I've got imposter syndrome." I think it's a good thing because if we went into a new role thinking we were the bee's knees, then we wouldn't learn and we would be arrogant and we wouldn't listen. And I think actually having that awareness of the things that we think we're not so good at is really, really important.

I really wanted to get her view on the complexities around visible and invisible disabilities. Diane replied:

When I talk to people who haven't really thought about disability, the things that they tend to think of firstly is that "it's too difficult" and it absolutely doesn't have to be and isn't. They also think that it is something that is present from birth and that's not correct either, because 83% of disabilities are acquired, so that's almost all of them.

They also tend to think about wheelchair users, certainly physical disability, but particularly wheelchair users. And I should caveat that by saying I think that's very, very important. It is actually ridiculous that we still haven't got it right for physical accessibility. That is something we should be quite ashamed of as a society.

*But leaving that aside, wheelchair users account for less than 10%
of disabled people; 90% of disabilities are not wheelchair users and actually the vast majority of disabilities are long-term health conditions,
mental health, cancer, and a huge range of conditions which are
not visible.*

*So, therefore, where is people's energy going? Is it going on trying
to work around a condition or concealing medical appointments or trying to find somewhere private to take medication or trying to work
around chronic fatigue or pain? And not telling you because they're worried about what you'll think of them if you do tell them.*

*If you can have a conversation with people and frame it as "What
do you need to do the best possible job?"*

*If I was going to say anything to anyone who wants to do some-
thing differently around their workforce and supporting people who
have an invisible disability, it would be – just when you're going to react
in a way that you might generally react, just take a moment to think "Is
something else going on?" before you react. That, I think, is the biggest,
biggest thing that can make a difference.*

This reminded me of a quote I use way too often, but
because it can't be heard enough – 30% is the time spent
worrying about trying to fit in for those in minorities.
Diane expanded on this.

*I think language also plays into this very strongly. I'm quite passionate
about this – businesses often use the language of disclosing or declaring a
disability, and that is so inherently negative. You "disclose" points on
your driving licence – or "declare" something you're bringing through
customs. It's really negative and secretive and implies there is something to hide.*

*Whereas if you just say, "Tell us what you need" or "Share your
story", depending on what the culture is for your organisation and what
fits, you immediately reframe it as something that is, at worst, neutral
and, at best, positive. And that makes a huge difference in enabling people to feel actually, it's safe.*

To me, diversity and inclusion mean value. We are talking about really valuing each person as a unique human being and creating an environment and a culture where everyone can flourish. So recognising that actually we need people from the widest possible background and skills and experience, and people's unique experiences and perspectives on the human condition, that's a huge richness to our lives and our work.

As a leader, I think it means living those values and creating that space where people can genuinely be themselves, however they want to be.

11

Winning Hearts and Minds

I remember the moment it happened so very clearly.

It was just after dawn on an almost-glorious British summer day, and I was driving to a meeting so important to the future of my company that I had an anxiety in my stomach that I'd not felt for a long, long time.

I could feel the all-too-familiar sensation of panic swirling round my insides. My heart pumping, my palms sweating, and my mouth dry. I was fighting to keep my hands from slipping off the steering wheel, as I desperately tried to breathe my way through the rising sense of overwhelm.

I was driving my husband's car, and for some reason the sat-nav kept crashing. The usually reliable voice in my ear telling me calmly how to get from A to B was nowhere to be heard, and the screen guiding me by its simple, bright colours kept disappearing to black. No matter how much I punched the button, the voice was gone.

As I started to feel the sense of despair rise in my chest, I found myself at a roundabout with no idea where I was supposed to go. I yelled at the sat-nav once more for good measure, praying it would kick in and tell me which direction I was supposed to take – guiding me to my destination rather than take me down a dirt track to a dead end.

As I circled the roundabout time and time again, the imposing signs telling me which route to take felt more and more alien as the words blurred and their meaning meant nothing. Tears blurred my vision as I saw my meeting slipping away from me – and I realised what a perfect metaphor this was for life.

We've all been there, haven't we?

Those days, maybe even lengthy periods of time, where you feel like you're driving someone else's car. . .that your internal guidance system is broken. . .that your options don't make sense and you're scared of getting in the wrong lane and taking the wrong road.

Sometimes we just feel lost.

We look at ourselves and we don't know who we are or where we should be going, and every time we try and follow the map, we end up at a dead end.

I'm not afraid at all to admit that I've had therapy for years and continue to do so.

Working through experiences, emotions, behaviours, and mindset is a challenging but rewarding investment in yourself. It could be that you've worked through the events in your life which have left you feeling scarred, scared, and limited without extra professional help – and that's truly incredible.

It could be you dip in and out of therapy as a sort of MOT, or a pre-emptive check-in when you find your emotions getting the better of you. Or perhaps, like me, it's been a lifeline which has helped you examine the puzzle of your life and help slot the pieces into place.

Like most people, my life experiences have been both positive and negative (sometimes simultaneously) and those experiences have impacted me in ways which I've needed extra help to process.

Being of a minority ethnicity in a predominantly white country has meant I have experienced racism. Some of it has been overt. Some would fall under "micro-aggression" and some stems from pure ignorance rather than explicit malice. That's not to say it's not hurt me, stayed with me, or shaped my own view of myself.

I've benefited from wonderful parents, a supportive husband, an inclusive working environment where I feel valued, and a pay packet which means therapy is available to me.

But not everyone has the support network for which I'm so grateful, and with the strain on NHS mental health services, being able to access emotional support is becoming more and more of a luxury. I've found this an uncomfortable truth as I know only too well what being "different" can do to our sense of well-being.

I've been curious as to whether how I feel about my own personal diversities is normal or not. And, of course, while any therapist worth their salt will comfortingly tell you there's no such thing as "normal", there are certainly patterns.

How does exclusion in the workplace, and in wider society, feed into our mental health and well-being?

In the 2023 DIAL Global Diversity Review, we found some fascinating results on both sides of the Atlantic. Taking into account the aftershocks of the pandemic, wars breaking out over the world, and the economic crisis, mental health is a facet companies can't and don't want to ignore.

We were pleased to see that there continues to be strong support for mental health provision in the workplace, with near universal agreement that employees have access to quality mental health care, and most companies saying they have a clear mental health strategy. Our member network has made it clear mental health is something companies will continue to invest in, as the risk not to and the implications this will have, not just on employees, but also on business outcomes, are far too great.

We've seen some impressive examples of best practice. Companies with the clearest strategy have a network of mental health ambassadors and first aiders, others give their employees dedicated mental health days, and others train line managers as part of wider well-being programmes so they can have the right conversations with employees and take care of their team. We are seeing more and more that organisations are recognising the positive impact of equity resource groups (ERGs) which are dedicated to supporting individuals with their mental health. In the UK, 86% of participating companies say they have a mental health strategy in the organisation, whereas in the US the number was 79%.

Almost all participating UK companies are keen to support their employees with access to quality mental health care (93%) and providing mental health training (78%). In the US, the numbers were 89% and 68%.

Where we saw a stark difference in the data was when it comes to tracking the impact poor mental health has on the business. Some 77% of participants dive into their data to track and monitor absenteeism, leavism, and presenteeism in order to understand the impact of mental health on the workforce and organisation. In the US, the number was only 38% – though it was up from 27% in 2022.

Jill Hughes is the MD for Accenture and is the executive sponsor for Mental Health for Accenture across UK and Ireland. Her passion for supporting teams with their mental health comes from her own personal experience when she was starting out in her career, as a consultant, travelling endlessly while planning her wedding.

One day I was back in the UK and was travelling into London on the Tube. It stopped between stations. The train was packed and I suddenly started to struggle to breathe. I started to hyperventilate. I felt I was going purple in the face, and honestly, I thought I was dying. It was just the most frightening thing, and I felt like everybody was watching me. What was probably three or four minutes in total actually felt like an hour. That was my first experience of having a panic attack.

I was not the kind of person that had mental health challenges. I'm not that person in my mind, so I didn't tell anybody about it. I pressed on to the office, and then the next time I was on the Tube, I had those same feelings again. And then it started when I was on a normal train, on a plane, and then in a traffic jam, and then in the hairdresser's. Then it's a party.

I just had this overwhelming need to breathe and get out. And all that time I kept it a secret. The one day I couldn't even get ON the train. I had to phone my boss, and amazingly, he got straight on the train and came to meet me at the station platform. The first thing he said to me, which was an incredible thing, was to say, "What you're going through is not that unusual." A wave of relaxation hit me and since then I've been a really passionate advocate of talking about mental health for many years.

One of the things that's been brilliant about being part of Accenture is that they really have a very strong mental health philosophy. I got involved in that programme right from the early days of joining. I became a mental health ally, I became a mental health first aider, then took over as the mental health executive sponsor. And I feel it's an incredible privilege to do that role and continue to really build this culture where it's safe for anybody to talk about mental health, where we can break down the stigma of mental health and really bring our whole selves to the work that we do.

Our mission for the work that we do is pretty simple, which is to make it safe for anybody to talk about mental health within Accenture and also to ensure that everybody knows where to go for help in that moment when you're suffering. We want asking for help to be seen as a positive step for all. We think it's very important for people to bring a very human side to the work that they do.

At the heart of our programme is this amazing group, our mental health allies – people that are working across the business in normal everyday roles, but they're a bit like the first line of defence. So that if somebody is not having a great day – they are feeling stressed or anxious in some way, they know immediately who they can talk to. We've now got nearly 3,500 allies in the UK and Ireland, and nearly 10,000 globally.

They are trained to have very open conversations with people, to listen as much as anything, because listening is fantastically important to connect with somebody when they're feeling isolated, low, and to point them in the direction of some of the support resources to help them strive and be at their best again. And we know that when people do get help, over 80% of the people who reach out for help say it's been very beneficial to them.

Diverse and inclusive leadership is about creating an environment where everybody feels that they can be themselves truly in the workplace. I think it's about encouraging that diversity and seeing the strengths of a diverse population. We know that diverse groups of employees are more creative and more innovative or more likely to create change. And I think in a business like our own, making sure that we're able to bring to our clients that diversity of experiences and viewpoints of perspectives and subject matter expertise is essential.

So, I think to do that, we need this inclusivity where everybody is welcome to bring themselves, whatever that may be, where it's encouraged that people speak openly, and you really feel like you can be yourself in the workplace, rather than having to wear a kind of corporate mask in some way.

Paul Farmer is the former Chief Executive of Mind. He stated:

The current environment probably puts more attention onto our mental health than we've ever seen before. Sometimes people think about mental health simply in the context of mental illness, but, increasingly, I think we're beginning to think about what we mean by looking after our mental health. In the course of the last year or so, we've often lost a lot of what we talk about as the "protective factors", the things that we do to really look after our mental health.

The more we understand that, the more we understand that we all need to look after, take care of, and pay attention to our mental health, and the better that will be for all of us.

Part of our whole purpose for being is to try to make sure that whenever it's possible, we create those channels, those connections, those links between people who are struggling, for whatever reason, and the help and support that are available.

People talk about their mental health as being sometimes like life. They've just fallen down a while and they're stuck now. All they can see around them is darkness and this tiny, tiny little speck of light up at the top. And our job is to literally drop the ladder down and say, just reach out, get onto that first rung of that ladder and we'll help and we'll try and pull you up a bit.

Our job is to make sure that people are not left behind. That is a big challenge at the moment because of the very real challenges that people are facing and for businesses, the wider society, and individuals.

We do a lot of work with employers and the genesis of that work started after the last crash where we started to think about the importance of the workplace from a well-being point of view.

Now we see many, many organisations, many businesses and public sector organisations, private organisations, and voluntary sector organisations really taking the well-being of their people seriously. I think particularly in this time, we've seen organisations who've come to the starting line of this crisis, having already thought about the mental health of their people, really investing in that, in a significant way, too, to good effect.

Diversity, inclusion, belonging, and equity mean two things. It means nobody is left behind, regardless of where they come from, what their background is. But, secondly, increasingly, it's about positively asserting the importance of a very broad range of diversity inside your organisation and inside wider society. And I think we've all got a job to do, both to create that environment, the culture for diversity within the organisation, but also to call out issues when we see them in wider society.

It's been inspiring to speak to so many leaders who are really putting the mental health of their employees front and centre of their policies. But one of the sectors where I've been so impressed by the fact that they put their head above the parapet is the world of sport, in particular, football.

I've had the pleasure of working closely with the FA and their Head of Inclusion and Diversity, Dal Darroch. Recently he chaired an event for us about whether organisations should be stepping up around the cost of living crisis and how surviving winter can take a huge toll on our mental health.

He told us: "Great strides have been made in terms of mental health issues being recognised and supported in the workplace, but those who normally don't suffer from mental health issues can feel the impact of the combination of dark days and, of course, darkness. Should leaders be recognising this widespread impact? Yes."

The session Dal hosted for us that day has remained with me as being one of the most powerful events we've hosted, due to the honesty and authenticity that the panellists shared of their lived experiences.

Geoff McDonald, who is the co-founder of Minds at Work, spoke about his personal mission to improve mental health in the workplace after a dear friend took his own life:

> *I left Unilever in 2014 to go out into the world, driven by a very deep sense of purpose, and that is to create workplaces all over the world where every single person feels that they genuinely, genuinely have the choice to just put their hand up and ask for some help if they are struggling.*
>
> *I don't think it's a very audacious purpose because in every workplace, anywhere in the world, if you had a common physical illness, you put your hand up and ask for some help. Yet, in the twenty-first century, there are billions and billions of people all over the world suffering in silence.*
>
> *Back in 2008, I got very, very ill with anxiety fuelled by depression, and the only thing that kept me alive in my darkest moments was my ability to talk. My ability to share how I was feeling, my struggles. What I got back in return were the two most powerful emotions in the world. One is called love, and the other one is called hope.*

That sense of love and a sense of hope were the two most powerful ingredients in my recovery. And so, yes, I slowly recovered. I went back into Unilever. And then in 2012, I lost a very good friend to suicide. And the night he died, I lay in bed and I thought, "What's the difference between him and me?" He couldn't talk. He was an alpha male – there's no way he could talk about his emotional and mental struggles. And instead he killed himself.

I lay there and I thought, "That's not fair." It's an injustice in the world, and I want to do something about it. And so I did some work in Unilever for about two years, and then I decided to leave Unilever and go out into the world, fuelled by a deep sense of purpose.

This is the kind of leadership that I find so inspiring – the epitome of a CEO Activist. Someone who has stared immense challenge and tragedy in the face, come out the other side, and then tried to make the path easier for the people behind them.

The story of Sandy Gold, who is the Chief People Officer at Pinwheel API, also moved me:

Diversity has been a passion for me throughout my career because when I was a kid, I was sick. My parents told me I could overcome that sickness and my siblings helped me develop superpowers to overcome it. That's when I realized that everyone had superpowers, and it came from their authentic difference.

So it became my mission in life to help people unleash their superpowers and see that those powers come from their diversity and their difference. As a young and now as a not so young, gay Jewish man, married to a black man, diversity has been in my life.

I do believe it's the responsibility of management to lead and provide support and allies on mental health.

I also believe mental health is also a superpower. It is that superpower to come to terms with reality and to shape it around yourself and express who you are. I think that we feel as we go through struggles, as we deal with reality itself, as we connect and create and construe our identity, we feel isolation.

We feel helpless. We need support. We search for meaning, and then we need community because we're both individual and collective. So I think when a company steps in and says, "We're on this journey with you," that's helping to solve for isolation. When a company steps in and says, "There are things you can do and we're going to help you with that," that's removing a sense of helplessness within empowerment when we create an ability to sense that someone's there for you.

Pauline Miller, who is the Chief Equity Officer for EMEA at Dentsu, was also on the panel that day. She shared:

Managements have a part to play in ensuring that our well-being and our mental health are supported. Individuals need to also take care of themselves. They need peers and allies around them, and the organisations need to put some of those organisational structures in place to enable that to happen. But we have to remember a lot of that is around prevention and thinking about how we maintain our mental well-being on a daily basis, on an ongoing basis.

There are times when we will see a lot of problems. We will find ourselves suffering from mental ill health. And when that happens, we need to think about the early interventions and then the post-interventions that we can put into place and that often very much relies on the manager and the organisation.

Geoff gave an incredibly impassioned plea on that particular session:

*Work can be brilliant. It gives you a sense of purpose. It gives you the opportunity to build relationships with people. You feel part of a community. It gives you a routine. These are all good things for our mental health. Yes, let's make sure there's support in place for people who might struggle like I did. But let's find a way of really shifting organisational culture where organisations **enhance** the lives of their people rather than diminish them.*

What does the culture look like? I think the culture looks like something where the way in which leaders are behaving is role modelling, enhancing their own well-being and therefore encouraging others in the organisation to use the resources to enhance their well-being. I think it looks like a culture where some of the systems, the policies, and the processes are there, about enhancing the mental health, the emotional health, the physical health of the people.

It's a culture where there's a sense of psychological safety, where I feel comfortable and able to talk about some of my struggles. It's a culture where there's a degree of peer support, where I can turn to a peer and have these conversations. It's a culture where there's a lot of listening.

Don't we want to just try – instead of having workplaces where we treat people as units of production – and create cultures where we treat people in the workplace as a unique and wonderful human being?

Sandy fully endorsed this message:

I worked at Yahoo for many years and it was one of my favourite cultures and there was a point where they let me create a job. It was about developing talent, developing leadership and communication across the company. I ended up calling it C3PO as there were three Cs and a P that were very important in the job. The Cs were collaboration, celebration, and community, and the P was for personal.

The culture in the environment really celebrated individuals. It made people feel psychologically safe. It lifted you up. I remember in 2015 when the Marriage Equality Bill passed in the United States, I went to my boss and I said, "Are you going to announce it to the company?" And she said, "No, you are."

And I said, "Why am I?"

And she goes, "Well, you're kind of the chief gay officer, so I think you should do it." And what I loved about that is she was celebrating things about me that were unique and individual, and I was in a company where that was being celebrated at a very important celebratory moment. You go to a place that amplifies you, that lifts you up, that celebrates the things that are unique about you, and then wants to hear your unique perspective and actually integrates that to the company and its identity and its view on the world.

While this is a phenomenal example of positive company culture, it's not an easy task to replicate it around the world. Guru Gowrappan – CEO of Verizon Media – has an incredibly interesting perspective:

When we are in the US or more developed markets, we can talk about these things – mental health, and even the idea that we can speak about stigma shows what spectrum we are on. But I think when you go into developing or underdeveloped country, or cultures, or society, I think it's a different story.

It's been very clear it's a critical issue on a par with physical health. It is raising awareness and normalising the issue of mental health. And I think that's important. And I think you're also seeing, at least again, back in the US, more and more companies are starting to expand their mental health offerings, which is great, but I do think there is a much deeper nuance to it.

How do you give them the right tools? How do you let people start talking about much deeper issues and being open about it and know that there's no ramifications negatively because they are being open about that? There's a lot more work to be done. A lot of it starts from walking the talk and making mental health a core part of our culture, which we have done.

We put that as part of the benefits programme for employers, and we are also making mental health a key part of our business because we know anything you do here is also good for business in many ways. But I would still say I think we've just started, I wouldn't even call it that. We are in the first innings. I think we're just warming up, based on what I see globally and from my vantage point, I always worry about the entire world.

We are on a mission to normalise mental health and advocate for a safe, supportive, and more inclusive workplace culture. We laid the foundation for a greater awareness and understanding around mental health and we led the tech industry.

We partner with experts. I'm an advocate for better mental health support at work. But again, I'm by no means an expert. We work with non-profits, have customised workshops for our executives, including one to really dig into mental health at the leadership level, ensuring our VPs have the resources and tools to help them manage needs for their teams.

My biggest thing is always to know that we don't know much. We all have natural biases and we don't understand that it's helpful to remove that blind spot and get experts – you don't have to be the expert, but find the right expertise, right partners for your organisation. Focus on education through conversation.

12

The Toughest Job of All

When we talk about CEOs, we can't help but think of business leaders and those shaping the country's economy. But we are all CEOs of our own lives.

Over the last three years I've been CEO of DIAL Global, CEO of my home, and CEO of my family. But in that time, it's been my responsibilities outside of work that have shaped me far more than the responsibilities in the office.

Do you remember when we started this journey together, right at the beginning of the book? I pointed out that while some facets of our identity will be with us our whole lives, many of our facets change and evolve.

When I first started the rough notes for this book, I was struggling to get pregnant and my parents, although having had health challenges, were fit and well. As I write this, I am now mum to an 18-month-old ball of energy, my beloved son, and I'm still grieving the loss of my darling dad – having helped care for him for the last few months of his life.

Both those experiences have shaped and changed me like no other. Throw in IVF and juggling the ups and downs of being a business owner, and you can imagine my stress levels of late.

As I'm sure you will have realised by now, I very much believe in authentic leadership, and have been nothing but honest about my personal situations over this tumultuous time. I've been very open on LinkedIn, for example, hoping that whatever I post will help others.

Losing my dad this year completely turned my life upside down and has left me a changed person.

I of all people understand that grief will swallow you whole, spit you right back out, and the world will continue to spin like it was nothing.

(continued)

(continued)

#GriefAwarenessWeek is a chance for employers to demonstrate their support in an area that most of us will experience at some point in our lives.

Sometimes, that process is relatively manageable (with "relatively" being the operative word). Some may need a couple of weeks off; others will need significantly more and will require continued backing and patience as they recover.

Other times, it can leave a person completely immobilised.

This wild variation in experiences means that workplace policies need to be equally flexible and led primarily by compassion.

Leaders, this week is your moment to bring up the topic and tell your employees that you are ready to give them the space and the security they need if and when this unfortunate fact of life comes around.

Grief is devastating; it can leave somebody a changed person. But with the right support, we can help one another to reach a better position to heal. ♥

The last few years, juggling being a CEO with being a mum, a carer, and a grieving daughter, has been excruciatingly difficult. And I'm not the only CEO who has been through such challenges. I've had the privilege of sharing the stories of some very impressive leaders who have put their own family struggles out in the open not only to help others but also to shape the policies of their own organisations.

Jenny Packwood is the Chief Corporate Affairs and Sustainability Officer for KFC, UK and Ireland, and played a key role in building the ESG offering of the organisation, starting 14 years ago.

"It's gone from being something that was really considered, 'we kind of need to do this purely because we need to have some nice things to say about ourselves as a brand and to give us cover with some of the more aggressive stakeholders out there' to 'this is a standalone function on its own that is strategically relevant and important to the business and it has a seat at the table at the highest level'. So that's something I'm proud of."

However, despite professional success, Jenny has had to deal with personal tragedy. She told us:

I turned 40, my professional life really kind of went into another gear. And I just found this kind of inner confidence, which was great. And at the same time, my personal life completely imploded. In 2015, my husband Darren was diagnosed with cancer, an aggressive cancer of his neck and back of his tongue.

Then we were strapped to this rollercoaster ride that no one wants to be on, one that you can't get off. And it was an incredibly, incredibly stressful time. We went through periods of the treatment itself. He went from being a healthy, strong, fit man in his early forties to looking like someone who was dying within a few months because of the brutality of the treatment.

He had chemotherapy. He had radiotherapy, and it was, it was horrendous. He wasn't able to eat. It was awful. The girls at the time were three and six. Life was honestly horrific.

He battled that for two and a half years and then he died in May 2018.

Through that time I had the responsibility. I was carrying the weight of his illness, the responsibility of being his main carer, and the responsibility of the children and being their main carer and having to be fit, healthy, strong for them, and to try and give them as much of a normal life as possible through this total carnage that was going on in our home at the time – and whilst working full-time and just trying to keep myself sane.

All of those pressures definitely tipped me over into not great mental health.

One of the reasons I have been so loyal to KFC as a business and the people in that business is that they were incredible during this period – this very, very dark period in my life.

My then line manager at the time was nothing short of incredible to me as a support.

I had about two or three chunks of time where I had to take just a chunk of time off work. And, of course, that put pressure on my team, that put pressure on the business. But there was never any sense that there was compassion fatigue coming from the business. It was just like, "We value you and we are going to be here. The job will be here. You need to just take the time to be with the family, to do what's needed."

I know there will be lots of people who might think, "Well, maybe if your husband had died and you had two young children, you maybe should have scaled your career back." But, genuinely, that never crossed my mind. Partly, because I love my job and I'm very motivated by it. And it's very validating for me, but also because I am now the sole breadwinner and I have entire financial responsibility for me and those two girls and I want to set them up for success.

I also want to be a great role model for them, because I'm a mother to two daughters and I want them to see what women can achieve when they put their mind to it.

I can relate to that so much – as someone who is trying to make their mark on the world as a CEO, as a mother, and of course, in memory of a father to whom I owe so much.

It's certainly not something I'm alone in.

In our DIAL Global Diversity Review, when we examined the facet of Parenthood and Caring Responsibilities, we found some fascinating data.

Companies who participated in our study continue to allow flexible working, a boost and relief for all, but particularly working parents. Some of the companies in our member network go further by rolling out wider job share programmes, giving working parents the opportunity to work 2–3 days a week, and sharing role responsibilities with someone else who works the days not covered.

Amazon UK, while often receiving negative press for working conditions at its warehouses, has recently announced it will start offering term-time working for parents and grandparents who wish to do so. This means warehouse employees can choose a contract that gives them

6 weeks off during the summer and another 2 weeks each around the Easter and Christmas school holidays.

According to CIPD, only 4% of UK companies currently offer this type of term-time working.

Three in four of the companies we surveyed have dedicated parental support beyond the flexible work that continues to be standard. This often comes in the form of parent training workshops, and ensuring line managers are equipped to support.

More companies surveyed now publicly state their offering for parental leave than last year, mainly to attract the best talent. Most of the companies we surveyed offer an increase in statutory maternity pay, with slightly fewer saying the same of paternal or adoption pay. This discrepancy in who qualifies for an uplift in pay highlights the need for parental policies to be reviewed, as many are outdated and focused primarily on expecting mothers, with some consideration to expecting fathers.

Understanding that family make-up is more dynamic, one company we interviewed recently updated its parental leave policy to include anyone growing their family, including expecting partners of any gender or sexual orientation, and adoptive parents.

Some 70% of participating UK companies say they publicly state their offering for parental leave (up from 52% last year). Almost 82% offer some form of an uplift on statutory maternity pay, with three in five doing the same for paternity and adoption (69% and 69%, respectively).

In the US, 81% of participating companies say they publicly state their offering for parental leave. Significantly fewer companies offer some form of an uplift on statutory maternity pay (68% vs. 97% in 2022), with further decreases seen for paternity and adoption pay (61% vs 86% in 2022, and 56% vs 70% in 2022, respectively).

And 74% of surveyed companies in the UK say they train line managers on how to support returning parents or those who are expecting (up from 55% last year). In the US, only 43% of surveyed companies say they train line managers on how to support returning parents or those who are expecting, and about the same number provide formal support for returning staff in the form of workshops, mentoring, or otherwise (47%).

Flexible working is embraced by most organisations we surveyed (92%) in the UK. In the US, 73% of participating companies say they offer flexible working to parents returning from leave (down from 86% last year).

Josh Partridge is the Head of EMEA, Yahoo. He offered this quote when we launched our findings:

> At Yahoo, we believe passionately that supporting working parents and carers is fundamental to the values of our company and we take that responsibility seriously as a leadership team. This commitment is not just limited to allowing time off for parental leave but also in providing a flexible work environment so that parents never have to feel like they're being forced to choose between work and family.
>
> As the leader in the UK, I am committed to leading by example, so when I leave work early to attend an event at my children's school, I make sure to share this with my team, so they know it's not just OK but encouraged and ensures every parent and carer feels empowered to follow my lead.
>
> This culture of support and flexibility is central to our mission of making Yahoo one of the best companies to work for in the UK and around the world. The company has a strong partnership with our Parents and Carers Together (PACT) Employee Resource Group, who are always sharing ways to improve our workspaces and working environment.
>
> This year I was proud to re-launch our "kids in the office day" over the school holidays as a great way for our children to spend the day at their parents' work, learning what they do and getting to meet the people they work with, as well as providing a full day of activities which in itself is a huge help for every working parent or carer during the holiday period.

Providing an excellent working environment and culture for our working parents and carers ensures we retain our top talent and has been key in attracting new talent into our company. I am also proud of our company's commitment to continuing to improve in these policies and put people at the centre of every decision we make.

It's imperative, to echo Josh's words, that employees can follow the lead of CEOs. I'm not the only one who believes this.

Citigroup chief executive Jane Fraser, who became the first woman to lead a major Wall Street bank, says bankers who want to balance raising a family with a high-powered finance career should "use me as an example". She was very vocal about flexible working not being dropped after the pandemic, and said while progress has been made on diversity in the financial sector, there is "a lot more work to do".

Roz Brewer is the former CEO of Walgreens. She too has led the charge on flexibility in the workplace. In an interview she gave while in the top job, she said, "We are learning one very important thing is the cost of day-care on young families. In many cases that is keeping women out of the workplace. And I think there are some solutions coming forward around affordable day-care."

When asked about a turning point moment in her career, she said:

Probably when I had my first child and I was a young mom trying to stay in the corporate setting, and it was a time where I was being tested. I was working for a gentleman who had already said to me he didn't think that I was smart enough to do the job that I was in, and now you're becoming a mom. And so that was his thing: let's think about you doing something else. And that was a turning point for me, because I set out to really prove him wrong, that, yes, I am going to be a mom, I'd held off long enough being a mom because of the corporate thing, and I was going to be a mom and I was going to prove him wrong. And I absolutely did, eventually.

He retired early and I actually assumed his role. And it took me probably 18, 24 months to do that, but I think my leadership showed up, my determination, my steadfastness, but also the appreciation that I was a mom, I didn't hide that I was a mom. I did all the things, I went to day-care and all of those things, but I did what I had to do. And it was a turning point for me, because I could have easily at that very point stayed home, be a stay-at-home mom, and believe what he said to me. And that was a turning point to believe in yourself.

Don't believe the hype of someone else that's looking down on you. And it charged me, and it still charges me today, and it makes me think about the young women in my organisation, and when they tell me they're expecting and I'm like, "Okay, let's get after it." That's fun. That's what you want. You want people to come work for you that have a fulfilled life.

And we're built around a family structure, so I want people to have a great family life. I don't want anyone ever to be told what they can't do because of what looks like might be an obstacle or a little break in time to stop them from being effective. I've seen people become actually more deliberate about the work they do because they have to parse out time. So I got better on my schedule because I knew I had to get to day-care to pick up a child, so I had to do 10 things before that, so it was disciplined for me. But that changed my life when he said that to me.

Gail Boudreaux is the CEO of Anthem. She told us:

We've provided 80 hours of paid time off for employees to care for parents or family. We launched a 24/7 concierge service and a confidential way for our employees to call, and it isn't just about work issues – they're calling about food insecurity, childcare, support for other health needs.

We rolled out a brand-new benefit called Papa On-Demand. It gives our associates 10 hours to use as they choose for rides or help with housework or scheduling medical appointments. We have been looking at health disparities for some time, so that wasn't new, but it was brought to the forefront with COVID, and then certainly racial injustice.

*We've worked extensively with Feeding America because food inse-
curity is one of the top issues. We launched a health plan for our own
employees, which is a life-essentials kit. They have a choice of additional
benefits around access to healthy food, transportation, and childcare.*

As a mother and CEO, I've been keen to highlight the
complexities of parenting and caring responsibilities in the
workplace, through our DIAL Global Virtual summits. In
2022, we addressed the issue of putting family fertility at the
heart of talent strategies.

More and more leading companies and organisations
are implementing family-centred workplace policies for
employees that span everything from maternity, paternity,
shared parental leave, as well as adoption, surrogacy, fertility, pregnancy loss, and menopause. And as companies
emerged from the pandemic, many felt this kind of shared
responsibility ultimately to "build back better" to ensure
that adequate financial and emotional support were in place
to protect employees' health and safety.

Sharon Peters, Head of Technology, Corporate Functions at Marks & Spencer, told us her journey started with
trying to get pregnant:

*I had five miscarriages over five years and now have two children. And
the struggle for me started with the first miscarriage. I told no one at
work – for lots of reasons, for example, "If I tell them they know we're
trying, if I tell people, they'd feel sorry for me."*

*I didn't want sympathy, I wanted hope, so I promised myself I'll
share my stories to give hope because when you're going through these
journeys, it has an immense impact on you personally and professionally.
And for me, sharing stories and reading others really inspired me to
make it much better.*

*I also remember seeing fertility specialists and trying to make sure
my appointments were outside of work and no one would find out. And
on one occasion I did get found out and I had to make these bumbling*

excuses. So now it's my part to play and create in the workplace where colleagues feel supported in every life moment and experience and fertility.

Kelly Phillips is the Head of Nursing for Fresenius Kabi. She told us:

It's my responsibility to encourage diversity within the workplace and encourage our managers to think about the importance of diversity when building that team, because this inevitably will enable more creative thinking, create a healthy challenge, and provide a greater richness of ideas.

It's absolutely recognised that organisations who have a clear focus on diversity and champion inclusion will undoubtedly perform better, have a greater employee engagement within their organisation, which for us, in turn, will lead to better patient experience.

Fertility in particular is such a difficult subject to embark on for many of our employees. It's really just as prevalent in both men and women. And I think perhaps men may find it even harder to talk about, particularly if they have a female manager. And so it really is about normalising conversations.

I just think it's remarkable that, as leaders, you know, we do tell our own stories because it is told with integrity. I think that encourages others to be honest and say that it really shouldn't be a barrier to employment. We absolutely should be facilitators and make sure that we can support them through that journey.

We also know that it has a significant impact on mental health. It causes a great deal of stress whilst people are going through this journey. And it's not a short journey. It's going to be that for some time.

Menopause is such an important topic for us; 90% of our workforce is female, about 40% of those within the 45–55-year bracket – retaining those valuable employees is essential. And it's recognising that these individuals are really either at the peak of their career or at the peak of their earning capability. And when you look at the statistics around women going through menopause, and it's still a taboo subject, some women still are afraid of talking about the consequence of menopause genuinely through the fear that it will affect their job.

I think it is important that we are seen to normalise those conversations. We cannot afford to lose women at that point in that career. We can't lose that talent within our workforce. I think what we're doing in the UK with nursing is normalising conversations and actually making sure that we're creating the right platform for those conversations.

Shirine Khoury-Haq is the CEO of the Co-op. She said, "I think if you're going to make real change and if you're going to stand in front of something and say that it matters or that things need to change, it has to come from the heart. And I think we've all seen people say the words but not walk the talk. And if you're not genuine, you don't get the results that you would hope to get."

Shirine is a mum of young twins, and as well as running the Co-op has been working with the Princess of Wales and the Royal Foundation on her work around Early Years.

This is a really formative time for children where so many of their future prospects are developed through the experiences that they have at that age. For me, it's important for a number of reasons. There was a lot of moving around in my life. The thing that I really had was a good grounding personally from that age, 0 to 5, and a good education during that time as well and through primary school. And then after that, however much I moved, there was a sense of stability and an ability to deal with things that were changing all around me. That kind of came from the core. And it's really important to me that we do build that within children in this nation. You know, you can't determine where you're going to be born. You can't determine which family you're born into which community.

However, what businesses and individuals need to do, in my opinion, is to do what they can to contribute to a fairer society and to be able to bring everyone with them.

I think when you add up the number of people that organisations of a certain size impact, whether it's through employing people, whether it's through serving their customers or in our case our members, whether it's what they do through community efforts, there is a huge impact that organisations can make.

But you do want to reflect your customer base and you need to be able to serve your customers, or members in our case, and I don't think you can do that without the diversity in the organisation and on so many levels.

I love DIAL's models for diversity because it's not just gender and race, it's disability, it's sexual orientation, it's socio-economic background, and all of these things intersect. None of us are really just one of those things. And I genuinely believe that you make better decisions, you produce better products and services if you have that diversity of thought within the organisation.

I think it is to be authentic in that activism and to really determine what it is that's important to you, that you feel you can actually stand up and talk about with credibility, both inside your own organisation, to be able to effect the change within one's own organisation, but also outside, whether it's in government or in media or other places.

It does sometimes put you in a place where you have stones thrown at you. I've been called woke, and you can't really explain it when those sorts of things come to you to say, "Look, I grew up this way. I grew up with people of all nationalities and all races and all sexual orientations and everything else. That's why I feel strongly about it." You just have to take it, but do what you can to impact as much as you can when you're sitting in in this chair.

I can't really impart words of wisdom. I have no right to try to do that. One thing that is key though is flexible working. One thing that we're really trying to do is ensure that everyone can bring their whole self to work, and in doing that well, flexible working is a part to ensure that people can have a home life as well as a work life, and be one person all the way through, without feeling that they're failing on one side or another.

I think it's important to notice what people are going through in their lives. So we've implemented a fertility policy, for example, something you and I can both relate to, and that applies to all genders. It applies to whether you work within the Co-op or whether your partner outside of the Co-op is going through a fertility treatment, or if you have a surrogate, so that you can be part of that journey, so that you can be honest about it at work.

But very importantly, to open the conversation about things like fertility treatment, about baby loss, about miscarriage, all of these sorts of things that I think people carry around with them at work. Everyone goes through one thing or another. But to be able to talk about that at work and to be able to have an understanding environment is key.

The menopause, for example, women are going to go through it. And, for so many years, women have suffered through it and haven't quite known what they're going through. And if you look at the stats, a lot of women drop out of the workforce because of the symptoms of menopause and the inability to talk about them. And we've been opening up that conversation as well, so that women can talk about it, so that men can talk about it, so the men can understand what their colleagues, but also people at home are going through.

We have a bereavement policy as well. People experiencing loss to be able to take the time out, but to have the support needed. And, for me, that's been an incredibly important thing that I feel that I can bring to this role. Some of it existed before. We've built on it, but it's so important to me that every last colleague knows that they're valued, that they're trusted, and that we care about them as a person, not just as an employee of the Co-op.

13

Love Is Love

If you've grown up feeling a little bit different, a little bit unsure of your place in the world and wondering if and how your whole, true self will ever be enough, then you will know how important it is to feel accepted.

It's something those who identify as LGBTQIA+ are only too aware of.

We may be living in 2024, but prejudice and exclusion are still rife.

The CIPD's most recent findings state "LGBTQ+ employees are more likely to experience workplace conflict and harassment than their heterosexual, cisgender counterparts. 40% of LGB+ workers and 55% of trans workers have experienced such conflict, compared with 29% of heterosexual, cisgender employees. In addition, a higher proportion of LGB+ workers (16%) feel psychologically unsafe in the workplace compared with heterosexual workers (10%), while for trans workers, this figure is even higher at 18%."[1]

Globally, we know the LGBTQ+ community face horrific challenges for simply existing in their true self. According to ILGA World, 69 UN member states "continue to criminalise consensual same-sex activity" and in 2020 there were six UN member states where consensual same-sex sexual acts are punished with the death penalty.

Closer to home, Stonewall released a report based on YouGov research – where over 3,000 LGBTQ+ employers discussed their experiences at work. More than a one-third hid their sexuality for fear of discrimination. One in ten Black, Asian and minority ethnic LGBTQ+ employees had been physically attacked by customers or colleagues in the preceding year; 38% of bisexual respondents aren't "out" at work.

The MHF also tells us a study from Stonewall revealed half of LGBTIQ+ people have experienced depression and three in five have experienced anxiety. One in eight LGBTIQ+ people between 18–24 have attempted to take their own life, and almost half of trans people have thought about taking their own life.

These are sobering statistics, and in the 2023 DIAL Global Diversity Review we were keen to see the results of our research.

Some 56% of participating companies told us they have at least one member from an LGBTQ+ background on their leadership team, up from 34% last year. Half of participating companies say their leadership has shared LGBTQ+ stories with the rest of the organisation (53%, up from 40% last year). Some 59% of surveyed companies, up from 41%, say their leadership team has approved an LGBTQ+ strategy in the past 12 months. Executive support has also increased, with 66% saying their ERG has an executive sponsor and 70% saying their sponsor meets with that ERG (up from 53% and 52%, respectively). And 58% say they gather and monitor data on the sexual orientation of their leadership team (up 35% over 2022), while 43% of participating companies in the UK ask if their employees self-identify as transgender (down from 47% last year).

In the US, 62% of participating companies say they have at least one member from an LGBTQ+ background on their leadership team, a significant increase from 49% who said the same in 2022. Some 59% of the US participants say their leadership has shared LGBTQ+ stories with the rest of the organisation, down 11% from 2022. And 66% of surveyed companies say their leadership team has approved an LGBTQ+ strategy in the past 12 months. However, executive support appears to be decreasing, with 73% saying they have a member of the executive team sponsor an LGBTQ+ employee network (down from 86% last year) and 71% of the executive team member meeting periodically with the employee network (down from 89% last year). Only 39% say they gather and monitor data on the sexual orientation of their leadership team, a sharp decline over 2022 (79%), and 38% of participating companies in the US ask if their employees self-identify as transgender (up from 24% last year).

Although sexual orientation remains in last place, significant progress has been made year-on-year with an index score increase of 15 points. This is apparent in the data with more participating companies agreeing they have a LGBTQ+ strategy (59%, up by 18%), have representation at senior leadership (56%, up by 22%), and outwardly role-model behaviour via story telling (53%, up by 13%). There has also been an increase in gathering data with regards to this facet, with 58% of participating companies saying they do so, compared to 35% who said the same in 2022.

For decades now, we have seen a steady increase in social acceptance of lesbian, gay, and bi relationships, and a steady increase in the percentage of the population who identify as LGBTQ+, meaning LQBTQ+ people are now more visible than they have ever been – in every community, and in all aspects of life. This means more lived experiences being shared openly and more employees from all walks of life feeling safe to be themselves.

But there is concern with the LGBTQ+ community for those outside of the UK, where safe spaces are shrinking, with geopolitics and global leadership challenges in the world are making this even worse. It is therefore down to businesses to create psychological safety for all employees, regardless of where they are. Almost all of the companies surveyed say they have an Employee Resource Group dedicated to the LGBTQ+ community. These groups are tasked with creating awareness, promoting inclusion and belonging, and identifying pain points and solutions within the business. More and more, one of those pain points is the use of language and explaining why words matter, such as using pronouns, citing sexual orientation instead of sexual preference, or talking to a group of colleagues instead of ladies and gentlemen.

I've had the pleasure of interviewing the superb Jonathan Lovitz, the Senior Vice President of the National LGBTQ+ Chamber of Commerce in the US. He told us:

> I joke often that I am so, so lucky to get to make my day job at my day job, the same thing. Because a lot of us that work in diversity, we have our 9 to 5 and then often our extracurricular work in diversity and various programmes that we work in. But it's my life's work and it's really wonderful that I get to do it day in, day out, all day.
>
> What I've loved working here and in the movement over the last decade is LGBT people are women, people of colour. We are immigrants. We are veterans. The work I get to do in this community is work that includes every community and ripples across every community. So for the last ten years or so, I've been working in LGBTQ and minority and diversity, economic development and opportunity primarily focused on public policy.
>
> I work in trying to get more laws passed that welcome and include more diversity in America, particularly in business. But I also do a ton of work on the political side. There's always good work to be done.
>
> I've worked in this space for over a decade and even though I'm an expert in the LGBTQ+ space, every day I'm learning a new acronym, I'm learning a new meaning. I'm learning that we're always on a dynamic spectrum of understanding here.
>
> Our diversity is our strength because I don't think anything can do more for moving our businesses and then, by extension, everything that business touches in our community more directly, than embracing the rich diversity all around us and even within ourselves.

When Jonathan addressed one of our DIAL Summit events, he was so clear about his vision for inclusion – from the ambitious to the seemingly small gestures that change everything:

> If it's not already in your work email signature, just adding your pronouns can do so much to let someone know you've taken the time to put such a simple, meaningful thing out there in the world for others to see.

And that is a spark that ignites much more conversations about inclusion wherever we are.

Most of the work we all do has been in binaries, whether it's the bathrooms in our offices or conversations. There's no need to assume we are all colleagues, we're all members of communities. So when in doubt, ask, we don't learn anything until we ask and research. So it's okay to ask folks, "How do you want to be identified? What can I do to help make things more comfortable for you in this meeting and in the way we interact?"

And it's sometimes as simple as just saying things like "folks", "friends", as opposed to "ladies and gentlemen", because there might be non-binary, there might be all kinds of folks in the audience.

I'm sure many of you have experienced that in your life, where you're not looking for anything more than just an ear or a shoulder. So start there. And then as you are comfortable and as the folks you're talking to are comfortable, continue your journey of saying, you can sometimes be at the back of the parade or doing high kicks at the front of the parade. But as long as you show up at the parade, everyone wins.

We're celebrating things like marriage equality here in the United States, but even with a recent High Court ruling here saying we're protected in some of our workplaces, we could still be thrown out of our homes. We can still be denied basic services for our businesses. So just because one major overarching victory helped me normalise our presence in some communities doesn't mean everything's fixed.

There's no such thing as a binary any more. And so you can have all kinds of variations up and down a spectrum, whether it's orientations or gender expressions or anything along that line. I talk about marriage equality a lot because it's something that is, I think, fresh in the minds of a lot of people, especially here in the States. And one of the things that I think was so great about it is the way that it was not about talking about, "Oh, those people want some special right or opportunity." It was framing it in a way that was very much about you and me. It was our kids' kindergarten teacher, our next door neighbours. Our friends would like to have the same things we do. Why would we begrudge anyone else that? So even in the office place where it still says 70% of non-LGBTQ employees say it's sometimes unprofessional to discuss orientation or gender identity – that's not saying you're talking about your personal life at work. It's just saying, "My husband and I went to the UK this time last year." I shouldn't be afraid of the context to say, "Oh my, my spouse, my significant other" – so much great research out there says anything we can do that makes a space more comfortable to take off that lead vest, as we think of it, lets you breathe the more easily.

We've had major strides here in the States. But nearly 40% of people say they've been openly harassed. This isn't some silent slight that happens behind your back. This is being called names. This is being openly berated in a meeting. This is being demoted because someone doesn't like who you are or how you love.

Nothing is more important than our visibility. And that doesn't necessarily mean wrapping yourself in the rainbow shawl and riding and leading the parade down the office hallway, although that could be a lot of fun. It's simply about making sure if you see, if you hear, a slight, if you see a room full of straight white men leading your diversity working group, we have a problem and saying something is the first step to addressing it.

Ignoring it is how we have situations where laws are passed and it still takes 20 years for hearts and minds to change.

I say this as a gay Jewish man with an invisible disability, there are many layers to me that you wouldn't know just passing me on the street, and all kinds of privileges that exist in my world help me overcome that. But I also know that my privilege to be a cisgendered white man invited to most rooms means that I have an obligation to scoot over in my chair to make room for someone who might not have been invited and making sure that everyone in the room knows that, while it's a wonderful thing that you thought to include me, we're not done yet and we'll never be done until we continue ensuring that everyone is there.

There are still over 60 countries where being LGBTQ openly is a crime, eight of them where you could still be sentenced to death for it. So we are changing hearts and minds around the world by conversing with one another about the power of business and opportunity.

How do we help young LGBTQ students, young Black students, young Asian students feel comfortable in their schools if we don't even have the most basic non-discrimination anti-bullying policies?

There are a lot of smart, talented people out there who are making an active choice to not work places or not be a contractor somewhere because they don't see what you stand for in defending families like theirs.

Don't just say we have a diversity and inclusion programme. Say that our programme celebrates everyone. LGBTQ+ – welcome. Asian – welcome. Black – welcome. You know everyone is welcome. Spell it out so people know that there is that place for them. Visibility like that is everything.

The companies who do it well, the companies who win the best of the best awards and who are out in front recruiting the best talent and doing tremendous work advancing diversity policy are the ones that remember there are 364 days that aren't the Pride march or there are 11 months that aren't Women's History Month or Black History Month.

You have to integrate these programmes into everything you do and to those thinking about their ERGs, remember to break down the silos. It's incredible that you might have the LGBT group meet on Tuesdays and the women's networking group meet on Thursdays, and your disability group meet every other Friday, but at least once a quarter, you have to put everyone in one room for a town hall or a network or some kind of event that says, "We're all in this together."

LGBT people in the United States alone spend $917 billion on goods and products. We are a discerning and loyal market and so are our allies. It says over 60% of LGBT people have changed the brands that they work with or that they shop with because of their known LGBTQ stance. Our allies pay attention to that, too.

Why would you spend your money on a company that is actively trying to hurt people when you could put it into a company that's actively trying to help?

When I see companies advertising their pink ribbon for women for breast cancer awareness, absolutely. I will choose to shop there in support of women, even if it's something as simple as my $2 cup of coffee. It's an act. It's an intentional act. It's a choice made to use my money to make a difference.

And that's what this report that we authored back in 2016 was all about, understanding economic impact. And we hope to do one of these about LGBT economic impact all over the world, because before this economy report, all we ever knew about ourselves was that we had buying power, which is great. It's wonderful that we're consumers.

But the impact in the community is as a GDP developer, as a job creator, and as a role model to shatter stereotypes. LGBT businesses in the States create $1.7 trillion, and that's despite the fact that we can still *be discriminated against. To put that in context, if LGBT businesses in the States were our own country, we'd be the 10th wealthiest in the world and I'd love to live there, the beaches would be fabulous!*

Nancy Kelley is the former CEO of Stonewall, but when she was leading the group, she appeared on one of our panels and had a profound impact on me. She told us:

Stonewall is one of the world's leading LGBT inclusion organisations, and really pioneered workplace transformation and inclusion. And when we do that through our diversity champions, work through the Workplace Equality Index, both in the UK and globally, we're thinking about the experiences of diverse communities.

LGBTQ people are not only their sexual orientation. We really believe strongly that essentially nobody's free till everybody's free, and that diverse workplaces are better workplaces for everyone.

We really try and focus on the experience of older employees, disabled employees, and people of colour. Working in organisations is part of all of the work that we do.

It's also really personal for me. I have lots of ways in which I'm privileged. I'm a white woman, for instance. I've got a good job these days, but I'm also a lesbian from a working-class background. Neurodiverse kind of. It's really important to me to be visible in all of those things, in all of these parts of my identity as a leader.

I think that's something that we also try and encourage leaders in organisations that are comfortable to be out about their own experience on their own identities, and that can be a really powerful way of kind of creating inclusive and welcoming environments.

I think that collecting kind of proper data around who employees are, who we are, is not so very hard. We support people to do really great data collection. We support people to do really great data collection on a global level where they're working in some contexts that are really problematic, where they can be forced to disclose LGBTQ employees' data. We think about "How can you understand who you've got in your workforce safely?" in those contexts.

I think there's something really important about the way in which diversity data arms leaders with the information they need to understand how they can get the best out of their colleagues, and how they can create the most effective, the most inclusive businesses. Mandating that at legislative level is a kind of whole other ball of wax. But I think as an employer, that's how we try to work. That's how we encourage others to work. And I've definitely seen it kind of transform our understanding of businesses at all scales.

This is about human beings. Engagement and talent and the experience of being at work, the experience of being a really creative, productive individual or really creative, productive team is a human experience. As leaders, we're wanting to support individual human beings, collective human beings to do fantastically well for themselves and for our organisations. And humans don't fit into one box. I think it's just recognising that really basic fact that our flourishing as individual people, our flourishing as teams, are absolutely about who we are and what we bring to work and who we are is never a single thing.

It's recognising all the people aspects of this that are really, really important. And we're all equipped to do that with or without data. We're all equipped to see each other truly and to value each other truly.

At Stonewall, we imagine a world where all LGBTQ+ people are free from harm, where we're embraced and included, we imagine a world where all of us can achieve our potential and we aren't just one thing.

We are people of colour. We are disabled people. We are old, we are young. It's an incredibly diverse set of communities that I'm privileged to be part of.

I would start by asking people if they can imagine the same world. Can you imagine a world in which your business is really successful connecting with communities and embracing the talent, the creativity that your colleagues can bring to the table?

Diversity is our reality. It's the world we're in, it's our customers, it's our colleagues, it's our suppliers, it's our communities. Embracing diversity isn't an add-on. Embracing diversity is embracing the world as it is. And no business is going to succeed in the modern world if it's not embracing both the reality and the potential of diversity.

We know that some kind of organisations reject that, where they try and stay really monocultural, lots of things go wrong. Those businesses fail to work with and welcome the world as it is. They struggle to connect authentically. And this is a real risk of kind of tokenistic engagement. But there's also a risk of shutting out whole communities, whole markets of customers, whole ranges of partners.

They'll find it hard to build talented, innovative teams. And that's not just about recruiting LGBTQ+ talent or talent of colour or disabled talent, because we know that inclusive employers recruit better talent across the board.

It's when leaders draw insight from the talents and perspectives of a diverse team when they're recruiting, developing, promoting people, they've got a very wide range of identities, of backgrounds and perspectives.

It's when we see organisations that really prize diversity within that workplace culture, and it's where we support managers to really embrace a really broad range of experience, the kind of "super diversity" and the perspectives that come from that diverse staff team, whether that's about age, class, background, culture, race, sexual orientation, disability, or neurodiversity.

We know you can take individual leaders and organisations who start from that place of cynicism, scepticism, to a place where they too can see that world. They can imagine that world where LGBTQ+ people are and where all people are able to live their lives fully. And they know those organisations are taking steps every day to make that world a reality.

Note

1. www.cipd.org/uk/knowledge/reports/inclusion

14

Age Is But a Number

Age in the workplace. Intergenerational workforces. How best can we protect our older team members, make space for school leavers and graduates, and navigate the huge differences between the five generations currently in our organisations?

It should be easier than we think – as several studies in Europe have revealed, businesses that employ an age-diverse workforce succeed better than those who focus on one age group at the expense of others. That said, we also know that CEOs in 2024 will be employing Boomers, Gen X, Gen Y/Millennials, Gen Z and in the next few years, Gen Alpha as well. So for CEOs to make this the asset that it is, they will need to think about how to bring out the best in everyone, and make everyone feel included.

Our 2023 DIAL Diversity Review offered some interesting insights.

Workers have experience and know how the company can support and nurture them to incentivise them to stay. Menopause is no longer a taboo topic, with almost all companies in our network saying they have a specific menopause policy, which can include guidance and training for line managers on how to recognise symptoms, have respectful conversations, and allow adjustments as necessary.

The UK has been especially hard hit with labour shortages since the pandemic. Those over 50 are re-evaluating their careers, the hours they work and many are retiring altogether. In fact, there has been a 9.5% increase in people aged 50–64 who are economically inactive, and there are 635,000 fewer over-50s in the labour market since the pandemic started. Given the wealth of experience and knowledge these workers take with them when they leave, it is no surprise that more and more companies are looking for ways to include those over 50 in their policies. In fact, more companies now say they have more specific age training for line managers on how to support age-diverse teams than last year, and more are setting up age-specific peer support networks or employee resource groups.

Our network of companies understands that flexibility, be it working from home, reducing hours, or taking time out in the form of sabbaticals is key, not just for older workers but parents and carers, those differently abled and those affected by mental health issues. However, fewer participating companies in the UK say they allow for reducing work hours or moving to part-time this year over last, and there has been a reduction in companies offering retraining for other roles.

Many companies now tackle important topics for this age group, such as feeling valued, approaching and planning for retirement, and menopause. Ensuring older workers feel they still have a significant contribution to make is key for many. One company we work with is conducting a diagnostic study focused on age to better understand the pain points older workers experience and how the company can support and nurture them to incentivise them to stay.

Work around the menopause has been impressive, as we've seen with ISS. Kat Parsons is the Head of Diversity, Inclusion and Belonging. She told us:

> As a business, we aim to address the complex issues around diversity, unconscious bias, and menopause awareness in the workplace with professionalism and sensitivity. This is achieved by providing information and awareness training to managers and the ISS Mental Health First Aider network. We are acutely aware the menopause is a difficult topic to discuss, both as the symptomatic person as well as the colleague or manager. There are also further barriers to consider, such as culturally shaped expectations about menopause, culturally influenced gender roles, race, socio-economic status, as well as transgender status. We strive to achieve

this by fostering awareness, education, and support and it is delivered through workshops, surveys, and other information and resources.

We found work flexibility is high among participating companies, with 90% saying they allow everyone to work from home, part-time or reduced hours (82%, down from 95% over 2022), allow the opportunity to change roles and/ or retrain (74%, down from 90% last year), or take sabbatical leave (73%).

In the UK, 92% of participating companies support employee well-being, such as having an occupational health service. In the US, the number was lower, with 76% – a significant decrease from 2022, when nearly all participating companies provided this service (95%).

Data collection on age diversity is high, with 88% saying they collect and monitor this data, up from 11% from last year. In the US, it's a similar number at 86%.

Some 72% of participating companies in the UK and 68% in the US have specific measures in place to reduce age bias in recruitment, as well as ensuring best practice sharing and learning across generations (65% in UK and 68% in US). An additional 53% in the UK and 61% in the US provide specific age training to line managers on how to support age-diverse teams. Some 39% of UK companies and 35% of US businesses say they have a peer support network for older workers and training specifically for older workers.

What I've been particularly fascinated by has been the sheer range of incredible work and insights being offered in organisations we're working with on a daily basis. From navigating intergenerational workspaces, to finding ways to tap into talent of all ages, to acknowledging the issues that each generation faces.

Thasunda Brown Duckett is the CEO of TIAA and is focused on ensuring Americans have safe and stable retirement. She has championed efforts to make saving easier and more impactful, especially for women and people of colour. I saw an interview with her in *Barron's*, where she explained simply what CEO Activism is all about. "At the core of what we do, we secure retirement. So what I'm excited about is doubling down on who we are."

And she's certainly doubled down on diversity, equity, and inclusion within TIAA. The "Retire Inequality" campaign highlighted the importance of acknowledging and closing retirement-savings gaps, but also amplifies the voices of women as well as now including a focus on the racial wealth gap.

If you think back to our earlier discussions in this book, you will have hopefully heard the message that when it comes to building an inclusive workforce, everyone needs to be listened to and heard. In a recent DIAL Global summit, we heard from Jack Parsons, the brilliant CEO of The Youth Group.

"I grew up in a council state. I remember going to school and getting laughed at because we couldn't afford a jumper, so for me, belonging and diversity are so important. I embrace it in everything we do. It's something I champion every day, and I don't want other young people across the world to ever, ever feel like I did. Growing up, lost, overwhelmed, and very lonely."

So, for Jack, negative and damaging stereotypes are something he seeks to call out:

I'm a big believer that you have to go from having all the answers to all the questions, and no-one has all the answers. We have to speak to each other and ask the question, "What does it mean to you?" Because at the moment I work with a number of organisations and I assume that they think they know what young people want, and also the young people on the flip side assume they think they know what the companies want. So there's a lack of communication. If you're both listening to the Taylor Swift song, one might be listening to it on an iPad and one might be listening to it on a cassette or a Walkman, and that's okay. You're still listening to the same song. It's about coming together and communicating more, not having all the answers and asking all the questions.

Then it goes down to compromise. The generations have to compromise between each other.

At The Youth Group, we've made sure that we've had multi-generational design teams when it comes to the job description, so the job description is not being read by an 18-year-old for a 55-year-old to join us. It goes round the table and everyone, every age, or every diversity group can get hold of it and break it apart and say, "Well, why doesn't this fit?" Or "You should mention this bit" and "Remember that people have got families and a lot of young people in my organisation don't".

The youngest changemaker is 18 and the oldest is 72. So it's a really diverse group of volunteers and supporters across the mission. Before, when we first started, the oldest was 24. It's because we didn't have the multigenerational focus on the job descriptions or on the opportunity when we posted them.

We focus on stage, not age. We should focus on the stage and the barrier they need to overcome. And then also look at the doorway that we're sending everyone through to apply for jobs and ask if it fits everyone.

Do they have access to a computer? Can they actually get online and actually use it, or do they use their mobile or do they even have a mobile to actually apply for jobs? So we have to look at that doorway and make sure that everyone fits through it.

Debbie Hewitt is the chair for Visa Europe, BGR Group, and the White Stuff. She told us:

I'm very passionate about agent diversity because throughout my career I've both benefited from leaders who really got the positives of age or diversity, and I've also been held back substantially by less effective leaders who didn't get it.

The benefits to having a diverse team are so easy and so obvious to me. You get more innovation when you've got groups of people who are different age ranges in an organisation. It gives a really positive message to your people. It's easier to recruit top talent because you can approach the senior stars, you can promote the young Gen Z.

If you've got that whole age range, it's such a positive message to customers. For the big brands that I work with, age diversity is a huge positive message to what your brand means and stands for.

The barriers are tricky because there are some very obvious, very hard barriers in organisations if you don't train people. Something like technology, if you're an older person, if there's not an investment in training, then you're going to be pre-selected out of that kind of organisation.

If you don't think positively, constructively, about mentoring schemes and don't make them happen, then it's obviously going to be barriers to attracting a diverse age range. I think the more difficult ones, all the intangible barriers start with leadership and culture. And very often leaders don't actually realise that they have got a sort of a subconscious bias against age.

Don't just look at the average age. Take the youngest and the oldest employee that you have in your organisation and ask yourself, number one, is that age gap reflective of your customers? Number two, look at your communications. Take the youngest and the oldest and ask them to say, is this good communication? See how differently they might react. And, number three, what are the symbols that recognise progress in this organisation? Again, take your oldest and the youngest and they will tell you whether you as a leader have got some kind of bias that you probably weren't aware of. Very powerful. A very quick and easy way to know whether you're part of the problem or part of the solution.

Ben Page is the Global CEO of Ipsos Mori, a trustee of the Centre for Aging Better, and someone DIAL Global has had the pleasure of working alongside many times. He states:

One of the reasons why I'm a trustee at the Centre for Better Aging is that if you look at the number of people over 55 that we employ, it drops off a cliff. And yet Europe is destined to be the oldest continent on Earth.

We are losing huge amounts of experience. And some of that is often a deliberate strategy in my industry, the media industry and advertising.

We walk around those offices and see how many people are over 50. And as a 55-year-old, I find it interesting. But some of that is about younger people being cheaper than older people. It's a fact of life and it's about how we manage people's careers.

One of the challenges is getting people to shift sideways so that the elevator gets crowded at the top. We need to be honest about that and look at how we can persuade people to not just leave because it's easier to get them to do that, rather for them to go into perhaps part-time roles or mentoring roles internally and going sideways, rather than just exiting people. That's the only way we can do that because we need those people.

We're short of workers in Europe and I think it's a huge challenge. It's been amazing, looking at people like BMW, adapting their factories, changing production lines for their older workers.

I think age is one of the last biases that is almost socially acceptable.

I think we need to look at the number of people employed and when they start disappearing. I can tell you, in many industries, it's long before retirement age.

There are lots of benefits having a long-standing workforce and my challenges with lots of experienced people who've been there a long time is how to keep reinventing and keeping things fresh, actually.

But of course bias in the workplace can work both ways. We recently held a summit session on "Unlocking Generation Z in the Workplace".

Serhat Ekinci is the Managing Director of Unite at Omnicom Group, and was keen to stress we should be wary of thinking about "obstacles". She stated:

I think it's worth a word of caution. I think about focusing on differences within generations. I think it's better framed and more realistic to talk about the differences in the life experience and the life context of different people. And I think that can often be completely irrespective of age or generation as well.

The biggest obstacle is probably the way people are thinking about these potential generational differences in the first place, which takes us to one of the core foundations of anything we do – it's about meeting people where they are, understanding who they are, and what they can bring, and then incorporating that into the experience they have working with and for you.

Carol Welsh is the former MD of Odeon Cinema Group and now CEO of AF Blakemore and Son Ltd.

When you bring together a team in a business, you're effectively also trying to get them to think about the customers that they're serving. I think it's really important that those age groups that you're serving are represented in your teams, because otherwise you don't get the breadth of understanding of how best to honestly inhabit what their needs are and how best to serve them.

A mix and a blend of differing opinions always make better sense than one side or the other. And the balance is always "How do you get people to understand the collective?" "What's best for the collective and best for the business?" I think it's about sharing openly, which is always one of our challenges, as leaders and also as colleagues.

Helen Webb is Chief People and Services Officer at the Co-op and once shared with us a fabulous phrase. She told us,

I worked for an American company, and it was common parlance to say, "We've got a really knotty problem here. We need some grey hairs on it" – actually referring to people with experience. So what is it about our society? We're not having a conversation about how experience should be valued.

We recently launched a managers' guide to the menopause, and we discovered that 52% of managers here in the UK have no idea how to support a woman in those circumstances or to even begin to have a conversation. Now, if you think about that 52% of managers and the diverse way they will be made up, it probably means that the majority of us as a nation have no idea how to have that, how to have that conversation. So what we've done is we've actually made our managers' guide to the menopause available to anybody who wants it. Any organisation can take it.

Jane Storm is Chief People Officer at Saga. She shared:

With any of these things, you never arrive and it's a constant journey. People talk about things like the career runway and "you wouldn't want to employ somebody over 50". Well, if you choose not to, you're missing the point completely. There's this whole opportunity for us to be keeping people in the workplace for many, many years. And it's very easy to keep people in the workplace well into their fifties, their sixties.

15

Getting the Full Picture

So far on our journey together, I've shared my experiences as a dyslexic woman of Chinese heritage, a mother and daughter, and CEO. We've read about the personal and professional experiences of CEOs as they focus and refocus their own kaleidoscopes, and how they move the DIAL to make the workplace a more equal and equitable place for all.

We've looked at the majority of the facets that my team at DIAL Global believe are at the heart of true inclusivity. But there are a couple of others that are key to note.

Socio-Economic Status

One of the facets of inclusion that is often overlooked is that of financial and economic inclusion.

We've been impressed with the steps taken by organisations in the UK and America to understand and fight against exclusion on economic grounds. We've seen improvement in both nations while carrying out our diversity review. Indeed, in the US, social mobility has quickly become the newest focus of many companies within our US network. Understanding that a focus on social mobility can unlock disadvantages for other intersectional facets such as ethnicity, disability, and gender, has galvanised companies to take a closer look, particularly given the current economic crisis.

As such, organisations such as Barclays are now including social mobility as a key strategic pillar for Diversity and Inclusion, meaning funds and resources are available to drive meaningful change.

Four in five of the companies we surveyed said they have specific outreach programmes to recruit talent from lower-performing schools or socio-economic backgrounds, a significant increase over last year. More are also removing

barriers to entry by removing university degrees as a requirement for entry-level positions.

Ray Dempsey of Barclays credits the UK with being
ahead of the US when it comes to socio-economic inclusion. He told us:

> *I think it's an enormous part of what creates differences – born on lived
> experience – that absolutely factor into what we think we can be, what we
> think we can pursue, and what we think we can achieve in our careers.
> The UK is certainly ahead of the US in the subject and a lot of the
> research and data that help us to understand how to drive it. We've been
> part of some of the efforts hosted by the City of London. There's been a
> socio-economic task force that Barclays was a key part of the research and
> the findings that linked to it, the data that shows that there are real gaps.*
>
> *My own personal reflections helped me to connect and to have an
> appreciation for why it's so important for us to focus. As a young person
> I didn't know a single person in my family or close to me that was in
> financial services. Financial literacy and the implications of a career in
> financial services were just completely far away from my thinking and
> my understanding.*
>
> *While it may or may not be a barrier, there's also a truth that for
> those who managed to get themselves into companies like Barclays, their
> socio-economic background sometimes is a factor in their ability to
> understand how to navigate through that organisation and ultimately
> achieve to the greatest of their ambition and their potential.*
>
> *Once we can close those gaps, there are still things that we need to do
> to provide targeted, focused support and development for people to under-
> stand how to navigate in ways that maybe they wouldn't have had a chance
> to learn by observation, or by hearing and learning from family and friends.*

David Martin is the former CEO of the Prince's Trust
and former chair of the Social Mobility Commission.
He stated:

> *I have spent a lot of time with people who I think would say they were
> at the wrong end of society, young people in prisons, young people on*

benefits, young people in countries who are having to hustle to make a living. And the sheer waste of potential just makes me weak, really. I spent my whole life trying to do something about it. I'm not sure I've succeeded very often, but it just is important. Without doubt, the good thing about globalisation is, I think, there is a chance to make things better.

The Social Mobility Commission in the UK has one responsibility and that is to bring out an annual report on the state of social mobility in the United Kingdom. And there's masses of research that goes into the document. A team of people that work very hard to produce it. But the bottom line is actually it hasn't really changed much at all, if anything, since the late sixties.

It slightly goes up occasionally, it slightly goes down. The thing that came up time and time and time again was really about self-confidence.

I'm sure you will remember the inspiring story of Jenny Packwood earlier on in the book. She's the Chief Corporate Affairs and Sustainability Officer for KFC, UK and Ireland, and has put ESG at the heart of her work – including the youth development programme, Hatch:

We all know that the pandemic exacerbated the inequalities in our society and actually young people suffer that the worst, and we are a massive youth employer. We know how to employ young people, we know what they need and basically what we were seeing was that young people, particularly post-pandemic, have been hit with so many negatives, and the areas of the country which were more deprived in the first place got increasingly deprived through the pandemic.

Those young people who were either socio-economically disadvantaged or they maybe were growing up in care or all of those things which give you barriers to leapfrog over in life anyway, had been shunted further to the back.

It was a whole cohort of young people, a whole generation that had missed out on two years of schooling. All of the things like youth clubs had been shut down. So those vital skills around social interaction, confidence, etc. had been lost as well.

We needed to address this issue around young people being left behind, youth unemployment. And so Hatch came about through that insight and it was about trying to tackle the issue that lots of young people want to work, but they don't have the experience to land a job or the confidence.

Next year we're hoping for 500 young people going through this programme and then by 2030, the goal is that 30% of our intake of our recruitment will be young people going through the programme. It's incredibly difficult to do. There are lots of barriers, like we are calling on the government to make it easier for employers to do the right thing by young people.

John Dutton OBE is the CEO of British Cycling. When I asked him which of the ten DIAL facets stood out to him, he said, "Socio-Economic Status. I think that the social mobility and social justice agenda continually get overlooked by the UK government and it is staggering that where you are born still plays such a pivotal part on most people's lives through lack of equal opportunities."

Ray Dempsey recently spoke at one of our events. He said:

There are two things about socio-economic inclusion we often overlook. They are two challenges faced by those who possibly see themselves as part of that community. There's the access. How do you get into a bank? How do you get into investment banking or financial services? Often people from a lower socio-economic background won't have family, friends, or connections who can help them understand that this is a real career opportunity. And while that matters a lot, there's another truth. People from socio-economic backgrounds will find their way into organisations and then really struggle to navigate.

When the 2023 Diversity Review came out, we asked for the perspective of one of the UK's leading CEOs – Jon Holt of KPMG. He told us:

We are committed to making KPMG a place where there's no limit to where your talent, achievement, and hard work can take you. Building an inclusive and diverse workforce is not only the right thing to do, it delivers better outcomes for clients, communities, and colleagues.

We have a long-standing focus on social mobility, from our work to raise skills and aspirations in local communities, to challenging our own recruitment and promotion processes. We were proud to be one of the first businesses to publish our socio-economic background pay gaps, while also setting ambitious socio-economic background representation targets for leaders.

Last year we went further, publishing the largest analysis of career progression by a business, which found that social class is the biggest barrier to career progression, compared to any other diversity characteristic. The pioneering study reinforced why we, and every UK business, cannot afford to overlook socio-economic background in our mission to bolster inclusion, diversity, and equity. This was an important step on our journey to deepen understanding of social inequalities in the workplace and drive change.

There's still a long way to go. That's why it's so important for businesses to work together, share best practice, and encourage others to join the conversation.

On the back of the review, we made the following recommendations.

- *Collecting data when recruiting*: Adding a socio-economic status question when you are recruiting is a quick and easy way to use positive action to help applicants from lower socio-economic backgrounds into the workplace. Such questions would include asking if a candidate was on free schools as a child, what type of school they attended, and what the occupation of the main household earner was when the candidate was 14.

- *Coaching and employee offerings*: It has been proven that people from lower socio-economic background need more coaching when entering the workplace. Often organisations will see these employees lack confidence, resilience, and lacking understanding of the political landscape of a working environment. Invest in coaching and mentoring to support these employees in the workplace to ensure they understand and feel their value to the organisation. Also consider offering more general life skills training, partnering with local experts to provide wrap-around support services, helping employees manage transportation, and ensuring better access to financial safety nets.

- *Enhance apprenticeship programmes*: Apprenticeships are a tried and tested way employers can drive socio-economic diversity within their organisation. Apprenticeships provide a unique solution to help attract people from a wider talent pool. Apprenticeship programmes can be costly and take a lot of work to understand, if you are a smaller business that wants to take part in an apprenticeship programme, find businesses similar to yourselves or larger organisations and see how they can support you.

- *Recruit with a view to upskilling*: A reskilling or upskilling model offers the opportunity for employees from lower socio-economic backgrounds to build new skills and increase value creation by entering into growing jobs and also exit declining jobs. In hiring, this can include identifying roles that require in-demand skills that can be learned on the job and creating a simple job application form. In onboarding, it can include front loading training on corporate norms and expectations and introducing peer mentorship; and, in the long term, it can include offering paid, on-the-job training and helping employees develop portable skills.

Nationality

I'd also like to reflect for a moment on the impact of nationality as a facet, before we wrap up our time together. Too often, the nuance surrounding this is swept up within conversations about race, and to do so does a disservice to both elements.

We live in a world that's getting increasingly smaller – and thanks to globalisation, the ease of travel, and our ever-connected lifestyles, it's more than likely we will find ourselves posted to a different country and/or working alongside colleagues from other nations and cultures.

In the UK arm of our DIAL Diversity Review, 84% of surveyed companies say they collect data on what countries their employees come from (up from 73% last year) and 34% of UK participating companies say they have 11–30% or less of their workforce from abroad.

In the US, 50% of surveyed companies say they collect data on what countries their employees come from and 39% of US participating companies say more than 30% of their workforce is from abroad, up from 18% last year.

After our 2023 review, Margot Slattery of ISS contributed the following:

In the workplace, people are our most important resource, many organisations say that. However, we really know it in ISS as we are a people-centred, self-delivery organisation and the people are at the centre of all we do. We are on our way to becoming a Company of Belonging and building this into all we do, as place-makers, we all feel the vital importance of this. So why doesn't every employer make it their absolute priority to attract, retain, and empower their people? There are a few magic ingredients: great leadership; changing the system from within; having courageous conversations; and being strong, and staying the course. But, ultimately, what we're talking about is having good diversity and inclusion and belonging policies.

To do this right, we must recognise that diversity and inclusion and belonging are more than a policy, more than culture, but fundamentally a physical experience. We need to engineer both organisational processes and the workplace itself. That means adapting to reflect the needs of everyone, offering different workplaces and break-out spaces, flexible working hours, diversifying our food options, and even providing reflection rooms and prayer spaces and acceptance of difference. The workplace must be an enabler; and, for that to happen, we need to understand the needs of our co-workers, regardless of nationality and ethnicity and race culture.

As we respond to the constantly changing and increasingly diverse make-up of our societies, there is still a lot to do. It won't be easy: there is no silver bullet, no one-size-fits-all approach, no blueprint for success. To move the needle, we first need to understand our marketplace, environment, and teams. Only then can you set objectives that are ambitious yet realistic. You don't change the world in a short space of time, but until we ensure diversity and inclusion and build belonging throughout the workplace, we will continue to devalue our most valuable resource: our people.

We made these powerful and accessible suggestions to organisations wanting to improve their rating on inclusion around Nationality.

- *Celebrate your organisation's breadth of culture and differences*: The best way to show your colleagues that you respect and appreciate them is by being open to the traditions and values of all cultures. This means avoiding promoting or embracing only one culture in the workplace. Every culture has its own feelings about work, authority, time, and what each person's relationship to the employer or organisation should be. Failing to understand or respect how these cultural priorities, such as time to pray or time with family, affect a team member's lifestyle can lead to an ineffective team.

- *Consider cultural training*: Spend time opening minds and changing mindsets, by educating your workforce about the different cultures of their colleagues. Think about more formal cultural training, dependent on your workforce make-up, to immerse the teams in the values and norms of the different cultures they will interact with.

- *Be respectful of language barriers*: A common challenge when working with different nationalities is language barriers between employees, especially if they have different mother tongues or strong accents. Remember to give those speaking a different language the time and space required to communicate effectively. Encourage people to get to know their colleagues beyond the surface assumptions by learning about their personal as well as work lives.

- *Set clear procedures to deal with tensions between groups*: If you employ different groups of workers who may be likely to disagree or to have misperceptions about each other, consider what procedures you have in place to deal with this. Do you have guidance on employing agency or migrant workers, making sure that they are not treated less favourably than permanent employees?

I was reminded of one of the fireside chats we had with the incredible Vismay Sharma, L'Oréal's UK and Ireland Country Manager. He's travelled the world in his 25-year career with the beauty giant and is well versed in learning to live and work within different countries.

When you start living in a country, every country's culture is multilayered. It's almost like an onion and you keep peeling layer after layer, skin after skin, and you have to really take time to go and visit consumers in their homes to understand what they do and why they do it.

You have to spend time in the field to understand what the retailers do, what the salon owners do, and, of course, a lot of time with the teams as well because you get brilliant insights from the teams. And if you're able to create a culture where people are able to express themselves, it becomes really, really strong and magical, because then you're constantly feeling there's a real exchange.

While you bring value because of your experience and your knowledge of the company, at the same time, you get a lot of value from people who understand the markets, who understand things that motivate the consumers.

I think it's so important that the modern leader of today really has got that international experience and the ability to actually communicate with lots of different people, lots of different layers, like you say, peeling off the skin of the onion.

When I speak to people who've worked in different parts of the world, I think when you get expatriated the first time in your life, you go through a bit of a shock, because you go to a place with expectations and then very often the reality and expectations are a bit different from each other, and that's where the shocks start setting in.

Once you start doing it on a regular basis, you move into a country with a very open mind, with this strong desire to listen to people, to understand why people do what they do.

People are clever everywhere in the world. There's a reason why they do what they do. There's a reason why they behave the way they behave. And if we go in with the humility that there is something I can learn from the situation, there's something I can learn from this culture, there's something I can learn from everybody I interact with.

I have to thank one of my bosses who I came across much earlier in my career, who said that "everybody that you come across in an organisation brings value and everybody has some good in them." And this is one of the key lessons that has stayed with me for a long time. That it stays with me even today and my very strong belief is, irrespective of background, of experience, of qualification, of gender preferences or religious beliefs or sexuality, I think everybody brings value.

Every single person brings value to the table. You just have to recognise the value. You have to appreciate it. And if you do that, and if you create circumstances for people to bring their best, they will almost always bring their best to the table. And that, for me, very simply, is diversity.

It's almost inviting people from different backgrounds to come and bring richness and to bring more flavours to what you want to do. Tolerance is the wrong word because tolerance means you're just letting people be, which is not the way it should be. You have to create circumstances which actually make people believe in a place, they believe in a cause, and they want to come and work for you and they want to give their best to you.

And that for me is true diversity, true inclusion.

My very strong belief is that what has helped me succeed so far is just absolute trust in the people that I work with. If a manager in today's world, which is becoming more specialised, more demanding, if a manager is able to create, to surround himself with people who are better at their jobs than he will ever be, he's fine. And that's what I have.

I have the leadership team of the UK and Ireland. I have a human resources director who's better at human resources than I will ever be. I have a CFO who's better at finance than I will ever be. I have a communications director who's better at communications than I'll ever be, and my job is not to do their jobs. My job is to create situations and circumstances where they can come and they can do their best. And, of course, I have to motivate them. I have to bring them together. I have to animate them and make sure that all of these people in a collaborative manner are working together. That's what I've done for most of my life.

The secret of success is the people you surround yourself with, because when you fall down, the people around you are the ones who are going to help you get up. And if you don't have the right people around you at that time, you're not going to get up.

It's quite simple. It's not rocket science. I think most managers, most successful managers, understand that. And this means surround themselves with people who are better than them. And I'm privileged that I'm surrounded by people who are much better than me at pretty much everything they do, but who also are modest and that's great advice as well.

What I know about authentic leadership – and authenticity is a term that seems to be bandied around an awful lot at the moment – is I have to be who I am at all points in time. I can't pretend to be somebody else, so I am who I am.

And at the same time, authenticity is also about how you translate into how you are with people around you, because there will always be situations, there will always be questions, and some of them will be difficult questions. And we have to act with full sincerity and as much transparency as possible, because you can't be 100% transparent all the time because there's always countries' confidentiality – but with full sincerity, we have to take decisions which are in the best interests of our people and our business.

Josh Partridge is the Head of EMEA, Yahoo, a leader who has left his native Australia, married a woman from another country and spent much of his career travelling around the world. He told us:

The modern leader needs to be someone that is able to cope with all of these different types of challenges, but also the cross-cultural pieces that are so important to understand properly, to be able to lead global communities and organisations. When you start doing business across a lot of countries, I think most people would presume that it's very different, from country to country – whereas I've always had the position that actually when you're working and travelling and doing your work in these different countries, I would argue that actually 90% we're the same.

When I was going to Moscow, I was talking to the brand manager of Pepsi, I was talking to the team from McDonald's, I was talking to some of the Russian brands there. And they're the very same, very similar conversations. They're all trying to achieve the same thing. Yes, the language is different. You've obviously got different backgrounds, but I would argue that we have a lot more in common than we don't.

Yes, we have different backgrounds, different perspectives, different educations. But even with that, we're still very similar. I do worry that the ability to have civil conversation and disagree respectfully, I do feel that side of things is diminishing. We're very much pulled into our own tribes and we need to be in that tribe, you've got to believe everything in that tribe and you've got to disagree with everything in the other tribe. And I think that's a really dangerous position for us to be in, in a democracy.

The reality is 50% of the population generally disagree with the other 50%. And that's always been the case. I think the ability to compromise has ensured that our democratic form of government democracy has worked. I think when you don't believe in anything and you look at the other side as the enemy, I think that's a real danger for democracy. I think we all have to really consciously be making an effort to bring a bit more civility back to discourse, to dialogue, because that's probably what I fear the most, actually, for my kids' future.

I think as a society, we have to take ownership at the, you know, at the individual level. I think we have to, as leaders, really show that compromise and listening are part of what as a citizen we should all be trying to achieve.

As a consumer now, I really want to make sure that I'm staying informed. Absolutely. But to try and limit my exposure to editorialisation of topics as much as possible so I can create my own, my view. But then again, my view is my view. It's that it's not going to be the same as everybody else's.

I think if you break down what is a leader trying to achieve – they're trying to get the best team, the best group of individuals possible to advocate their particular product or service into a market.

There's two sides of that. One is around attracting the best. If you limit yourself to a certain group of people, you're limiting your ability to attract the best. I think from just a purely capitalistic view of labour, that makes no sense, right? You need to ensure that you are taking the best talent from the biggest pool possible.

The best way to attract the most diverse and the biggest consumer pool is to make sure your messaging, your services, your products are attractive to the biggest population, the biggest group of consumers. So even from the most basic view of capitalism, you know it makes total sense.

Whether you believe in CEO Activists and whether you believe in the politics of it, if you strip that away and just look at the pure common sense from a business perspective, leaders should be trying to attract the best talent from the biggest pool of candidates possible.

From a human perspective, as leaders, it's our duty to ensure kids have the best chance of succeeding in life. And my job as a parent is to give them a platform so they can make that decision, and they can strive for whatever they want.

I think as a society, we should be the next level down – parent to society is the same thing. We want any little kid waking up to feel like if they put the hard work in, they can achieve whatever dreams they have, and I don't think it's controversial to say there are a lot of kids waking up and not even knowing what potential they have or can only see one or two avenues to having what you would want to call a successful life.

I think as a society, we have a challenge and a job in front of us to make sure that as many kids as possible feel like they can achieve if they work hard, and they're committed, they can achieve anything.

There shouldn't be anything artificially blocking that route. I think from a leadership point of view and something that we can do right now is, we can lean in, we can make sure that our teams are achieving the first challenge of making sure that we're getting as diverse and attracting the best talent from a society, so we can drive that thinking in our companies right now.

Let's start with what we can do. And what we can do is make sure that we are making sure our workforce represents the consumer or that the audience we want to target, but also what can we do to expose younger people to the careers and that are available for them in our industry?

I've been very, very lucky to have also worked for some really great bosses who were very supportive of me and my career, and I think for any leader, you definitely need those sounding boards. Everyone needs those people that they can confide in, to go to for advice, use as a sounding board. And I've been very lucky to have those people along the way. But again, through sounding boards, through good confidence, they will also give you that feedback as well.

And you need to be big enough to be able to take it.

Conclusion

I have to admit, as I put the finishing touches to this book, I'm feeling really rather emotional.

Finding my place in the world has been a long journey.

Navigating running a business has been a rollercoaster.

Analysing my experiences, the learnings of others and formulating the words to adequately convey just how important my quest to "sort out the FTSE 100" (as my friend Lord Woolley once joked) has been overwhelming.

How much of myself do I give? Do we all have to publicly share all of our thoughts, fears, and vulnerabilities to be an authentic leader? Do we have to fight for every cause in order to be a true CEO Activist?

The answer to this of course is clear – being an authentic leader means answering those questions and acting honestly on your decision, no matter what that is.

Looking back through my life with the experiences I've had and lessons I've learned has helped me put some events to bed, heal some traumas, and turn my back on painful interactions. I've been able to reflect on what has made me the Leila I see in the mirror today, take my own personal kaleidoscope and twist it round and round to get the clearest vision yet of who I am, where I've been, and where I'm going.

For me, doing the work I'm doing in this space has helped put the challenges I've had into context so that I can put negativity in my rear-view mirror, move the DIAL for change, and clear the path for others to have an easier journey in the workplace and society.

I've also been so honoured to have met and worked alongside some truly incredible people.

I mentioned Lord Simon Woolley earlier. I still find it staggering that I get to work alongside trailblazers such as he, and that he looks to the work I do with respect. It humbles me more than I can say.

And as we enter another year filled with global and economic uncertainty, we need good, authentic leaders more than ever. As I've said many times through these pages, I've had the good luck and the honour to work alongside some deeply impressive leaders, and I wanted to include some of their final thoughts here.

I'm reminded of the brilliant words of Diane Lightfoot from one of our many inspirational summits on disability. "Ultimately, wouldn't it be great if as a society we got to a point where we didn't need labels at all and we just saw everyone as individual human beings who are unique with unique skills and all equally valuable? The whole idea that you have to sit in one box or another is patently ridiculous."

Tinisha Agramonte is SVP and Chief Diversity Officer for Disney. She's a humble powerhouse of a woman and I love her. Her advice is simple.

Lead by example. I try to be the change that I want to see. So that means, first and foremost, I recognise that these conflicts are rooted in our belief systems, our value systems. These are beliefs that we hold firmly and they're deep and they're emotional. They're not rational or logical. So when we try to have conversations of understanding with people, they end up being debates because we feel like we're being personally attacked for the ways that we were raised, the things that we were taught, and we learn.

So the first thing I try to do is have compassion and empathy that we have all lived very different lives. We have vast experiences, and those experiences are rooted in our social identities, our race or ethnicity, our national origin, our socio-economic class, all of the things that you can think about that we differ as human beings.

Lord Simon Woolley, after one of our summits on how leadership changes in politically and socially divisive times, made the point we're echoing in this book – that it's crucial for society to "believe in themselves to be transformative, to play that role, to own that leadership space and win, for we inspire".

"It's emotional. It is. It's clear that these things are getting an emotional response."

I mentioned moments ago that the world needs good leaders more than ever before. I'm not talking purely about leaders at podiums asking for our votes, and, despite what this book is about, I'm not talking only about leaders in boardrooms.

I'm talking about you. Whether you lead a business or a Scout group, whether you're a CEO or stay-at-home parent – we all have a crucial role in life, in our communities and on this planet.

Someone who knows from first-hand experience just how important it is to work as a community when fighting for change is the brilliant Paul Gerrard, Campaigns, Public Affairs & Board Secretariat Director at the Co-op Group. A former civil servant from a tight-knit community outside Lancashire, "co-operating" is practically in his DNA. But he knows leadership – in whatever form – isn't always easy.

It's a question of resilience. You've got to accept not everyone will agree with you, not everyone will like what you're doing.

I think there's also a point about honesty with yourself. You might think something is right. You genuinely believe that, but if you're maybe coming up against people saying, no, you've got to understand why they're constantly saying no.

Maybe it's that you think they're wrong to say no, or there's a vested interest, or maybe they're protecting something and there are negative reasons for that. But understanding them allows you to either say "no, I'm right", or "you know what? I probably need to change as well."

There was a time, and I think it's changing, when our leaders couldn't say you had got that wrong – because if you did, it made you look weak. I think the willingness is now to be open and say "maybe there's a different way."

I began this book by defining what we mean by diversity. I want to end it with some comments I shared at a recent speaking event.

"Diversity to me means being Chinese. Being adopted by White British parents. Recently understanding the immense journey of caring responsibilities as well as also the loss of my dear father. Each and every one of these life experiences I carry with me, and I take into the workplace in order to hope and drive better change for our future generation of leaders who don't just care about role models, but they care about real models as well. And that is diversity. Diversity is every single one of us."

There's no question that talent is everywhere. I truly believe everywhere we look, we will find talent. But opportunity isn't. And it is our responsibility to step up and take accountability not only because we know it's the right moral thing to do, but because it truly is an economic and social driver, a commercial leader for prosperity. Now, and for the future generation of leaders. But it starts now. With us. With our organisations. With our voices. We must not just put our voices, our hearts behind it, but we must measure and put that data in place to make real sustainable progress and change.

The pages of this book are packed full of insights from people in top jobs who are determined to make the world a fairer place, and I hope you've been able to harness these words to inspire your next steps as you go out and "be the change you want to see in the world".

I'd urge you to remember, though, that you're not going to get it right every time, and you're not going to be perfect. I tell CEOs all the time that they shouldn't be afraid of tackling the DIBEC agenda just because they're afraid they're going to get it wrong.

We are works in progress, and aiming for perfection is a fool's game. We will have days when we do absolutely feel like we've got life nailed. And there will be days, if not long, where we don't. The point is, we're trying our best, showing up and working towards being and doing the best we can.

We also have to remember to seek out those who already love and accept you. If you've spent your life to date feeling on the outside, you may be used to "going it alone". I'm here to tell you I'm living proof that's just not the case.

I plummeted to the pits of despair when I thought I had to see myself though one lens and not many. I was isolated when I listened to and accepted stereotypes surrounding my heritage, and I turned my back on the people who were protecting it.

So look, really look, at the people in your life and who seek to lift you up and support you. Who listens when you talk, when you cry, and when you laugh? Who tells you to apply for the job you think you couldn't possibly do? Who checks in on you when you've been too quiet for too long?

When you've assessed who your support network is, don't doubt them. Don't overthink it. Accept them, because they accept you.

No one ever gets it right the first time. I've particularly loved, as well, being on the learning journey. I think it's, you know, whatever phase we're at in our career, we are always learning, learning, diversity, inclusion, belonging, equity. Culture is a living, sleeping, breathing piece, and it's something that will never be complete.

I'm a business owner, wife, and mother. I'm an advocate and speaker and I doubt myself no more. Nothing is won by me hiding in the shadows and not making my mark in the world.

The world needs us to play big, so step up, let's do it.

Starting Dial Global with the unwavering belief that talent is everywhere, and opportunity is not. This early shot was in my living room with a homemade studio where the business was founded.

Stephanie Mehta, CEO & Chief Content Officer of Mansueto Ventures, parent of Inc. and Fast Company, and me. Stephanie has been a role model to me for many years and I admire her hugely.

Aki Hussain, Group CEO, HISCOX, Non-Executive Director, Visa Europe, and me at the HISCOX Offices in London.

The Unilever Unmissable Awards with trailblazing women, Aline Santos, former Chief Brand Officer & Chief Equity Officer, Sinem Kaynak, Chief Growth Officer, Beauty & Personal Care and Leena Nair, CEO, Chanel.

Tami Erwin, Former EVP & CEO Verizon, Board Director, John Deere, F5, Xerox, York Space Systems and Skylo and an Operating Partner for Digital Gravity

Ramcess Jean-Louis, Chief Diversity Officer, Pfizer and Alvie Tremoulet, Global Diversity, Equity & Inclusion Lead, Pfizer. I was kindly invited to keynote at the Annual DEICE council forum in Rome

At Verizon Headquarters with Sandy Gould, CPO, Pinwheel, Christina Schelling, SVP, Chief Talent & Diversity Officer, Verizon and Traci Sanders, VP-Global head of DE&I, Verizon.

DDR UK 2023 Release at London Stock Exchange

CEO Activist at No 10 Downing Street - 18th May 2023

CEO Activist at No 10 Downing Street - 8th June 2023

Peter and me recording an episode of the Diverse and Inclusive Leaders Podcast!

Dean Curtis, Chief Executive Officer - LexisNexis Risk Solutions, Data Services at RELX, NED, Trustee & Advisor, signing our CEO Activist pledge at the House of Commons

Jhumar Johnson, Chief of Staff, The Open University and Ben Page, Global Chief Executive Officer, Ipsos and me at a CEO Activist event at Yahoo Studios in London.

I love these giant letters!

Outside Number 10 Downing Street having hosted a roundtable discussing diversity as a commercial lever for economic growth and prosperity with CEO's and C suite from leading national and global businesses.

At NYSE celebrating the launch of the DIAL Diversity Review.

NYSE celebrating the launch
of the DIAL Diversity Review
with Participants and Partners.

Hosting a panel at the DIAL Global Summit with Alicin Reidy Williamson, Chief Diversity and Culture Officer, Yahoo! and Elly Tomlins, Chief People Officer, Britvic.

Shirine Khoury-Haq, Group Chief Executive Officer, Co-op, and me filming one of the first episodes of "The CEO Activist" Podcast

Speaking at Canon Medical UK's employee conference in Sheffield

Julia Hoggett, CEO, London
Stock Exchange Group and me
at a celebration of 50 years of
women on the trading floor.

The team and I, with participants of our DIAL Global Mastermind Council, kindly hosted at Colliers.

"Our mission is to help you to do well by doing good. We help organizations to grow and innovate by building inclusive cultures"

Leila's portrait

Index